S0-AJH-881

A NEW SONG

Pat Boone

CREATION HOUSE
CAROL STREAM, ILLINOIS

A NEW SONG © 1970 by Charles Eugene Boone. All rights reserved. Printed in the United States of America. No part of this book may be used or reproduced in any manner whatsoever without written permission of the publisher except in the case of brief quotations in articles and reviews. For information address Creation House, Incorporated, 429 St. Charles Road, Box 316, Carol Stream, Illinois 60187.

FIRST EDITION, AUGUST, 1970
SECOND PRINTING, OCTOBER, 1970
THIRD PRINTING, NOVEMBER, 1970
LIBRARY OF CONGRESS CATALOGUE CARD NUMBER: 75-131441

Acknowledgment

New Testament quotations are taken from *New American Standard Bible New Testament* by permission of Lockman Foundation, LaHabra, California.

CONTENTS

AUTHOR'S PREFACE

I see a grave danger in telling this story. Many may feel that we see ourselves as something "special," because God has blessed us as He has. You may suspect, too, that we offer our experiences as a basis by which others' devotion and relationship to God may be judged.

Oh, friend, please believe that this is the very last thing we want to do. We can't judge anybody; your relationship to God is between you and Him. We simply share, in great joy and humility, what He's done for us. If it inspires you to seek more of the living God, in your own private way, in your own solitary time with Him, this book will have achieved its only purpose. We are not criteria for anybody else; we, too, are searching and seeking more of Him.

So we commit and dedicate this effort to the living Jesus — and pray that *"He would grant you, according to the riches of His glory, to be strengthened with power through His Spirit in the inner man; so that Christ may dwell in your hearts through faith; and that you, being rooted and grounded in love, may be able to comprehend with all the saints what is the breadth and length and height and depth, and to know the love of Christ which surpasses knowledge, that you may be filled up to all the fulness of God.*

Now to Him who is able to do exceeding abundantly beyond all that we ask or think, according to the power that works within us, to Him be the glory in the church and in Christ Jesus to all generations forever and ever. Amen.

Ephesians 3:16-21

INTRODUCTION

In the entertainment profession, I catch a good bit of guff from my colleagues: Dean Martin, Phil Harris, Andy Williams, Don Rickles, Frank Sinatra, the Laugh-In gang and others. Let's face it—I am an oddity.

Don Rickles, known as the "Insultan" and "The Mad Mongoose," because of his double-edge tongue, at various times has called me: "Mr. Clean." "Pat Bland," "Goody White Shoes," "The Teen-Age Billy Graham," and a lot of other things that will never make it to the time capsule.

Once, Phil Harris and I were together on Andy Williams' show. "You know, Pat, I never had a son," he said.

"But if I had, I'd want him to be *just like you*. . .until he was three years old."

Dean Martin and I have hacked up some songs and golf courses together. Not long ago, in his mock-serious 100 proof way, Dino cracked a new one.

"That Pat Boone! He's so religious! Y'know, I shook hands with him the other day and my whole right side sobered up!"

I laugh now, but not long ago I was cringing at these epithets. Although they're really compliments, they cast me in the role of a square, a guy just a little bit out of the mainstream of life. And I was starting to wonder, myself.

As I wondered, I wandered. My marriage, my family life, my faith, all began to unravel in the classic tragic pattern of today. The more I tried living in two worlds, the more I found myself pulled apart.

5

Then something happened to me. I discovered something more important to me than my public image, or anything else. My relationship with the most significant person in all history—Jesus.

Up to this time I had been a churchman, paying my dues. I'd been investing regularly in the institutional bank: church attendance, contributions, and all the test. The "treasure" was accumulating in my heavenly account all right, but I was afraid to write checks on it. In other words, I didn't know how to claim the promises that Jesus makes in the Bible to those who'll believe Him.

The trouble was, I'd lived in God's house 21 years without meeting my landlord! I knew a lot about him—but now I've met Him!

I've discovered that Jesus Christ is as alive today as He was 2,000 years ago when He walked the dusty roads of Galilee. And man, when you experience His living presence, not just intellectually but in your very spirit—*you know it.* And so, my life has changed.

My friends in the entertainment profession are colorful, vital people! We have a great time together. But most of them couldn't quite figure me out, even before this change!

For instance—Phil Harris. He asked me once: "Pat, you don't drink?"

"That's right."

"Not nothin'—never?"

"No, Phil, nothing."

Turning to the studio audience, Phil said, "Can you imagine waking up in the morning and knowing that's as good as you're gonna feel *all day long?"*

Everybody howled, including me.

It wouldn't have done any *good* to have said that I feel great when I wake up—now, more than ever.

This book hasn't been easy to write. In fact, some chapters have been downright painful. I would rather have left many things unsaid many failures and flaws hidden away. I really would rather my own daughters not read this. But time is short; the world is sick; families are disintegrating; people are crying out, searching for answers. They're turning to drugs, sex, rebellion, mysticism—and even Satanic worship and witchcraft.

Many of the things that have happened to us, you'll find hard to believe. So do we, sometimes. But people are finding the Bible hard to believe, too.

6

Most of the excitement in our lives has come from discovering that the Bible is as current and immediate as today's newspaper—and a lot more accurate. It should be; it was programmed by the same Heavenly computer that hung the stars.

A word of warning: a host of Christians, ministers and regular members will be shocked and aroused by our discoveries. I'm fearfully, and prayerfully, aware of the controversial nature of our experiences. But they are experiences—not theory, or hearsay, or wishful thinking, or psychological fantasy. They're life-changing experiences.

Churches today are in a terrible crisis: young people are rejecting organized religion. They're not buying the comfortable, dogmatic, lethargic, impractical, unweildy, clannish groups that meet in fancy buildings. They're looking for God! The God of Abraham, Moses, Peter, Paul and Christ! The God of action, of change, the God of now! What the Holy Spirit is doing today is disturbing—disturbing in the same manner that Christ disturbed "organized religion" and the world 2,000 years ago.

Above everything else, I've tried to be honest. It's been an excruciating, soul-searching, God-seeking effort. I pray to God that each reader will suspend judgment until the story is told and then search the Scriptures independently and prayerfully to "see if these things be so."

For us, from our search, they are so.

The living Jesus has brought great joy, great faith, great hope and confidence, great over-coming power to our house and into every crevice of our lives.

I sing a new song today. I rejoice in the psalmist's exultation, "O sing unto the Lord a new song; for he hath done marvelous things: his right hand, and his holy arm, hath gotten him the victory.

"The Lord hath made known his salvation: his righteousness hath he openly shewed in the sight of the heathen" (Psalm 98:1,2).

Beverly Hills, Calif.   Pat Boone

Thank you, Father,
for the seven richest human blessings of my life.

Daddy

Mama

Shirley

Cherry

Lindy

Debby

Laury

CHAPTER 1

HIGH ADVENTURE

A light breeze crept up Coldwater Canyon in the Hollywood Hills that memorable afternoon. Earlier in the day it had pushed the sludgy pall of smog over the rim of hills that encircles the city of Los Angeles. Now its freshness washed our faces like palmfuls of cold water.

To the north, the San Fernando Valley reached out through the suburban sprawl to softly undulating hills and then sloped down to the plain where the great ranches begin that are marketbasket to all the U.S. To the south lay Beverly Hills, Hollywood and the flat delta-like spread of Los Angeles itself.

We shaded our eyes to look to the west. There the blue Pacific stretched toward the horizon and shimmered like a huge mirror in the blazing sun.

We had gone up Mulholland Drive to this lonely spot on a crag above the road—a black-shirted and white-collared minister and I. Back down in Beverly Hills a friend of mine had brought Harald Bredesen to the house for a visit. After awhile my friend excused himself, saying he would return later. We chatted aimlessly for a time, then Bredesen suddenly said, "Can't we get outdoors where we can pray?"

Pray outdoors? I hadn't done too much of that. But I like to be out in the sun.

"Sure," I had said, "there must be a place up Coldwater Canyon. I'm not quite sure where, but let's go."

Soon, we parked the car beside the road.

"How about up there on that point?" asked Bredesen. I agreed and we headed for it.

"Let's run," said Bredesen. "It helps to clear your mind."

As we ran Bredesen started to pray. Out loud!

Something else new, I thought. First this youthful appearing, enthusiastic minister wanted to go outdoors to pray. Now he says we should pray while we run. I tried to concentrate on what he was saying as we scrambled over the rocks, scattering the birds before us.

Below us now the wonder of God's creative genius and the ugly scars of man's attempts to overpower nature clashed in a cacophony of sight and sound. But had I fully known the deep and abiding spiritual experience that would be mine in the next few hours, the view as I saw it would not have been nearly so impressive. In hours to come it paled into insignificance—in comparison to a new relationship with God that I had never realized was possible.

"Every man wants to know God."

When I first heard that statement I wasn't so sure.

In my world, the entertainment business, I was sure I knew some people who didn't. On the surface these individuals didn't indicate any interest in God. In fact, judging by what they said, oftentimes they were angry at God. But then I recalled occasions in unguarded moments when these same people had expressed to me some of their deep concerns. Inevitably these anxieties revealed emotional or spiritual overtones.

Only the other day I had been in New York City with an

entertainer known to millions through his radio and TV appearances.

"Religion is only a crutch," he said. "It's for the weak-minded people who are afraid to stand on their own two feet and take life as it is."

We were caught in a traffic jam on our way to Madison Square Garden. The taxicab inched along. "I believe God intervenes in our lives in many ways—even when we're not aware," I ventured. "Take your illness. . .don't you believe God pulled you through that?"

He hesitated a moment. "Oh, I received thousands of letters. Yes, hundreds of thousands of letters from people who told me they were praying for me. I appreciated it, and said so. . . ."

He laughed. "But it was a gutsy surgeon who really saved my life."

But the crack in the facade had already appeared. For all of his bravado, I couldn't escape the feeling that my friend was only trying to cover up the chasm of longing which every man knows who has not yet found God.

Back on the hilltop the minutes stretched into hours. As we talked the sun sank lower. Now it hung just over the horizon paving a path of molten gold across the water.

In astonishment I watched and listened to Bredesen. It was difficult to tell when he stopped talking to me, and when he started to pray to God. He prayed with his eyes closed. He prayed walking. He prayed standing still. He also knelt down to pray.

The sense of God's presence began to grow on me. The sun dipped into the ocean. Darkness crowded over the hills to our backs. Lights winked on in the houses in the valley below. Only faintly was I now aware of the physical world about me.

All my life I had been fairly religious. As a boy growing up in Nashville, I never missed Sunday School and church. After I married Shirley Foley, daughter of "Red" Foley,

11

widely known country and western singer, we attended church regularly. In fact, soon after we were married, I had preached for the Church of Christ in Slidell, Tex., for about a year, while I was at North Texas State College.

Every now and then, I thought about becoming a minister. But when an entertainment career blossomed unexpectedly, I felt I'd been given an opportunity to demonstrate that a man could live a Christian life no matter what his profession might be.

Still, like so many others today, much of my concept of Christianity was doctrine, a set of rules to which I subscribed and which were supposed to supply the answers to the problems of life.

It hadn't worked; I still had my problems! As an adult with a family there were perplexities to which I had no answers. Moreover, I could see that my inability to come up with solutions was beginning to affect my family and our relationships to one another.

But weren't these normal for a person in the 20th century? I thought so. And I consoled my wife, Shirley, saying: "We may not have all the answers right at the moment. But if we just hang on I'm sure things will work out in the end."

Actually, life had been kind to me. Without much training I had done exceptionally well in the entertainment field. Along with the success had come sizable sums of money. This, together with a wife who loved me, and four healthy daughters, should have made me a happy man. Naturally easy going, I was usually able to dismiss the imponderables with a shrug. "It'll work out all right," was one of my favorite sayings.

But sooner or later, to every man, come the haunting questions, "Who am I? What am I supposed to be doing on this earth?"

Philosophically, I had answered these questions. Basis for these answers I found in the Bible, and the record was plain: God had created man. His purpose in doing so was

12

that man might worship Him, serve Him, and eventually enjoy eternity with Him. This was basic Christianity. I had accepted it intellectually, and to the best of my ability by faith had acknowledged Jesus Christ as my Savior.

But what was happening to me on this hilltop? Never before had I sensed the nearness of God as I did now. Never before had I prayed as I was now praying.

Later I recalled the experience of Saul after his call from Samuel to become king of ancient Israel.

According to instructions, Saul was to go to "the hill of God" where he was to be met by a group of prophets.

The Bible says, "And when they came to the hill, behold a company of prophets met him; and the spirit of God came upon him, and he prophesied among them."

Up to this point, my life had been quite a normal one. Except for another great spiritual experience of several months before, which I shall describe later, my religious life had been that of the average Christian. As a matter of fact, I considered myself to be several cuts above the normal church member. In my professional career, especially in the early years, I had turned down TV opportunities and parts in motion pictures because I didn't believe they were consistent with what I saw my responsibility to be as a church member.

Faith in God was a very real part of my life. At home we had family devotions in which my wife Shirley and our four girls all participated. We attended church Sunday morning and evening; we were always present at prayer meeting Wednesday evenings. Yet never before had I experienced the sense of the Lord's presence as I did now on the mountaintop.

I had the feeling He was all around me. With the sense of His presence came also a feeling of release—as though I were suddenly freed from the restraints and limitations of the world below me. Jesus had said,"You shall know the truth, and the truth shall make you free." Many times I had quoted that Scripture. Now I *felt* it—from the very soles of my feet to the top of my head.

We prayed; we talked; we wept together—two men who had never met before and who knew little or nothing of one another's background. Yet we were worshiping God in a unity of mind and heart that seemed always to have existed. I sensed a love for my brother and for my wife and children in fact for all those who came to my mind in those hours, that I had never sensed before. Was this the love of God the Bible talks about, the very reality of God Himself? I wondered.

By now the blanket of darkness covered us. Only the stars looked down on us in our moment of sublime reverie.

How easy it was to picture King David as a lonely boy on the hills of Judea watching over his sheep by night. I could almost hear the words of his song.

The heavens declare the glory of God, and the firmament showeth his handiwork. Day unto day uttereth speech and night unto night showeth knowledge. There is no speech nor language where their voice is not heard.

We prayed. We wept. We shouted. We sang. It seemed to me that all the inhibitions, apprehensions and concerns of my life were washed away. Those haunting spiritual restraints that somehow had kept me from reaching out to God as I desired, disappeared. I reached up to heaven with my arms aloft. Not to touch God, but to give myself to Him.

I had never done this before. Many times in my life it had seemed to me that my prayers had bounced back from the ceiling of whatever room I was in. Not now. Every thought seemed to penetrate the heavens to the very heart of God.

The breeze of five hours ago now had crept on over the hilltop and wasted itself in the valley below. From out of the canyons around us emerged a chill blanket of fog. The time had come to go. Yet the aura of the presence of the Lord was so real, it was hard to think of leaving.

14

What had happened to Pat Boone in those past five hours?

In the next few pages I'd like to relate the events leading up to this, and then share with you the exciting experiences that have been ours since then.

This is no new philosophy of life. No! It's a relationship with the Lord *plainly described in the Bible,* but one which many people like myself, faithful church members and devoted Bible students have simply overlooked.

CHAPTER 2

WHERE TO GO FOR HELP

The other day I spoke at the Sunday morning worship service of the Church of Christ in Monroe, La. I may have shocked the overflowing congregation that morning; I hope so.

"Isn't this ridiculous? We could have stayed in bed and slept this morning," I said. "Instead we came over here to this building where we've closed the doors, sung songs and prayed—as if we actually thought someone was going to hear us!

"We passed bits of bread and cups of grape juice around as if they had some significance. When we get through here we're going to go out thinking that somehow or another we are better fitted for the tasks of the week, which will have no relationship to what we've been doing here.

"Not only that, but some of us will no doubt attempt to persuade other people to join us in this silly charade!!

"What's more (and this must be the *most* incredible of all), we have taken money out of our pockets which could have been spent on other things to help maintain this beautiful building in which to play this shadow game!

"When you stop and think about it, it's an absurd thing to do, like kids playing school on the back steps. . . . That is, *unless we really do believe that God Himself is in this place,* that He does know our thoughts and answers our prayers."

The psychologists tell us that this "exercise in futility" is our search for an emotional crutch. Man doesn't feel competent to solve his problems. He would like to think that he has a big brother somewhere who will come running when the problems get too big. Although we've come so far, so fast technologically, we would still like to retain a childlike faith in the reality of God.

However the psychologists may describe our dilemma, we are aware of the fact that we are living in an impersonal world. Increasingly everything we do is related to punch cards, credit cards and numbers. And simultaneously, we are faced with the most serious problems man has ever known. Our faith simply doesn't appear to be equal to the challenge! Church services seem completely out of context with the world we live in the other six days of the week.

I've grappled with this problem myself.

Beginning five years ago or more Shirley and I would be in bed, the lights would be out, and she would say, "We're supposed to be a Christian family. We start our day with a prayer at the breakfast table and we have devotions with the girls before they go to school. We have prayer at night and the girls take turns leading that prayer. And yet we don't *actually study the Bible together.* We don't *really* pray together except a couple of minutes a day. Maybe this is the reason we don't have answers for a lot of today's problems, we aren't doing anything to find the answers."

I had to agree, but I had taken the attitude that when the time came or the showdown was at hand, we could work it out some way or other.

Years went by with Shirley occasionally sort of nudging,

and sometimes pleading, for me to take the lead. After all, I am the "head of the family." I'm supposed to be not only the financial provider, but also the patriarch, the spiritual leader of the family. But I wasn't even looking for answers *myself,* much less for the answers for members of my family!

Sure, we'd go to church, but my children would have to punch me to keep me awake. Since I'm not by nature a big worrier, I can go to sleep quickly and soundly. *One day I almost fell over sideways!* Then, in desperation, I discovered that I could not fall asleep while I kept both feet off the floor, because of the physical effort involved. That's a tough way to get through a church service, but it worked for awhile.

Many other men, I discovered, are faced with this problem—especially those who go at a fast pace all week.

When we sit down in a church service, we know somebody is going to preach a sermon. We know we're going to sing songs we've sung many times before. We've done this so many years that we can predict what the next move will be without opening our eyes.

I had many friends who said, "I just don't get anything out of church."

One man who is involved in government, a bright and dynamic guy, said, "The minister will start out enthusiastically talking about the problems of the day. He gives the impression that he's got the answers. I listen and think, 'great, man, now I'm going to hear something I need.' But when he finishes he still hasn't given me any practical advice on how to solve my problems. I keep thinking maybe I've missed something somewhere. If he gave the answers, I didn't hear them. I walk out with a feeling of disappointment, an emptiness and sort of frustration, because like everybody else, I would like to think that God knows who I am. I would like to think that if He has the answers He'll help me with my problems."

To be honest about it, I think many people—even fine

19

church people—are saying to themselves in the privacy of their own rooms, "I'm not experiencing much that's worth talking about in my spiritual life."

It seemed easier a couple of decades ago to come out of a church service, pat yourself on the back and say, "Well, I've done my duty to God this week."

Today the problems are so enormous that church attendance—or even participation in a church and Sunday School program—is not enough. Even educators, business leaders and statesmen admit that the dilemmas of our day are staggering. Obviously we need more than human wisdom. Sir Winston Churchill before his death said, "Our problems are beyond us. We are a generation staggering around the rim of hell."

Plainly, the answer lies only with the Lord.

In the first three or four years of my career as an entertainer I was aware that God was doing something with my life. I couldn't explain it in any other terms, because a hit record in those days was a sort of miracle, and two or three in a row was unheard of. Yet for several years practically everything I recorded sold a million or close to it and went right into the "Top Ten."

In almost unbroken succession came "classics" like *Ain't That A Shame, Tutti Frutti, I Almost Lost My Mind, Don't Forbid Me, Friendly Persuasion, Bernadine, Love Letters in the Sand, April Love,* and many others.

I had to make difficult decisions early in my career. I had just moved to New York City to appear on the Arthur Godfrey show when I was offered a television show of my own. It was to be sponsored by a cigarette manufacturer. I was only a college student at Columbia University, married and with our second baby on the way. We needed the money. But I asked myself the question, "What does God expect of me as a Christian?"

When my agents saw I was hesitating they said, "You're not selling the cigarette, you're just singing the songs. Let the sponsor sell the cigarette."

But I couldn't escape the obvious fact that the sponsor wouldn't be hiring me if he didn't think I was going to sell his product. I said, "No."

At this my manager and agents shook their heads. "This guy is out of it. He just doesn't understand the entertainment profession."

I agreed with them. I was simply trying to get through school at that time and was grateful that God had given me a couple of hit records to pay my tuition; I was planning to be a school teacher, anyway.

Then another sponsor came along. This was a beer sponsor. It took me even less time to say no to him.

"Well, we can quit concentrating on this guy because he's not long for this business," my agents said, and again I agreed.

But while I was still a student at Columbia, Chevrolet wanted to sponsor a half hour musical show with me as host.

The agent gingerly approached the subject, "Got anything against Chevrolet?"

"No, I'm driving one now," I said.

So I went to work for Chevrolet and the show was on the air for three years! That first year, 17 other musical variety shows went on the air. Mine was one of the five or six that survived, and yet I was the youngest and least experienced of any of the performers!

Yes, I had a certain sense that God was guiding in these things. And I was trying to make my decisions based on Christian principles.

After college, I graduated from TV to movies. We moved to California, and my career became more and more important. I began to feel more secure in the entertainment business, and felt that I had earned a place in it. By then I had made 13 gold records. I also made some movies that were big successes, and did occasional TV specials that had high ratings.

Meanwhile, our children were getting older. They were

starting to ask questions that were difficult for us to answer.

"Mommy, our teacher said that we're all descended from monkeys. Is this true?"

Or one of their friends would laugh at their serious belief in Bible stories and they would ask, "Is it really true, Daddy? Did they really happen?"

And then of course they would come home with dirty jokes they had picked up at school. When they went to church with us we saw that they often were much more concerned with giggling with their friends, drawing pictures or doing their homework during the sermon.

What were our answers supposed to be? I read the Bible, but I really didn't study it for answers to such problems. I went to church services, but I would often sleep through them. I would lead singing once in a while, even teach a Sunday School class. But none of those helped a lot.

In the quietness of our bedroom, Shirley would plead with me.

"Pat, when are we going to read and study the Bible as a family? We need to know what He wants us to do."

I would say, "You're right." Then I would be asleep.

I had the feeling that I was doing as well or better than the average guy. I would say to myself, "I'm putting in a few more hours in church than others, and God gave me this career. But after all, He's not my agent so I guess He intends for me to use my own wisdom, my own judgment about maintaining my career. After all, I've got to keep this career going so I can help God out in my spare time."

Then I liked the idea of being able to say, "Yes, I'm a Christian and able to be a good influence in a more and more amoral industry. It's not easy, but it can be done. I may compromise a little, but the over-all effect will be good."

I wasn't alone in this attitude-trap; I've discovered that this is a pretty common attitude among Christian business men today. We're great middle-of-the-roaders. We take pride in the parts we play in our industry or profession;

22

and—we're often proud of being Christians, too. Yet sooner or later, when the chips are down, we don't know how to handle ourselves. I was to discover this later to my own sorrow.

For now, we were greatly disturbed at what happened to one intimate friend of ours. He was a neighbor in New Jersey who held a responsible position with a large airline.

Weekends he spent puttering around the house, playing ball with his son, helping his other children with their homework. Theirs was a real "All-American" picture. The one thing that this family was missing was a relationship to God. Shirley and I would talk to Ed and his wife about it sometimes, and invited them to go to church with us.

One day he said, "You know, we've tried to give our kids everything we think they need. But I guess the one thing we haven't given them is a faith in God, and maybe we ought to do something about that."

So they started going to church with us. As they read the Bible, they believed God and became members of the Church of Christ. This was great. . .at first. But right away, there was more than an hour consumed just driving back and forth to the church from where they lived in New Jersey. Ed was a conscientious man with a good position. Since he and his family had all become believers, he was soon selected as a deacon.

Now his Sundays were spent differently. He drove into church for the Sunday morning *and* evening services. Deacon's meetings and prayer meetings took him away from the family circle once or twice a week at night.

Then a calamity occurred. Two airplanes went down in New York City. As a representative of the airline his responsibility was to go to many of the more than 100 families and express the sorrow and condolence of the airline and offer to help. Confronted with this tragedy, his work load, his church duties, and the virtual loss of his family life, he suffered a nervous collapse. As his wife told

23

us, he was putting a great deal into the church, but not getting much out. Now, confronted with the problem of providing comfort and encouragement for others, he discovered he didn't have the emotional or spiritual resources necessary. He stopped gcing to church completely.

In this hollow, empty period we couldn't understand why God permitted something like this to happen. We realized that if we had been in Ed's place. . .we wouldn't have had any more answers for these people than he did!

The incident appeared to heavily underscore the fact that just "belonging to a church," simply attending church services, *will not equip you for the calamities and shocks and problems waiting for you down the road!*

Certainly, I believed there was a God. I believed that the Bible was His Word. I knew from my study of the Bible that there are a lot of internal evidences as well as external evidences that it is true, archaeologically as well as historically. I knew of the fulfillment of prophecy and the harmony of the Bible itself written by some 40 men over a period of 1,500 years.

Did I believe in Jesus Christ? Of course, I believed in Jesus because if I believed in the Bible and the Bible talked about Jesus and in the fulfillment of prophecy, I *must* believe. And yet, at the same time, I was disturbed at the many "moral" people who flourished and achieved and made a great deal of money. They were good people, good to their families and appeared happy in every way. Yet they had no particular faith in God and didn't participate in any church activity.

Shirley would weep over them. We wanted to talk to them about their lack of faith in God, but we didn't know how. *We didn't have anything to talk to them about!* They seemed to be just as happy in what they believed as we did in what we believed.

We could not point to very much in our lives that was different from what they experienced. This was a hopeless feeling. If these dear friends of ours are as misled and under-nourished spiritually as we believe they are, why couldn't we talk to them?

"How can we go about our business, earn a living, raise our children and never talk about the Lord to our friends, the people who are the closest to us?" Shirley would ask.

And still. . .bringing up differences in doctrinal beliefs with our friends seemed almost impossible. To do so would threaten our friendship. And as we had so little in *our* lives that was different from what *they* had, there appeared to be no point in doing so.

We could explain thoroughly the doctrines of the church. I could quote all sorts of verses from the Bible. In fact, the Lord had given us the privilege of helping a number of people to become Christians, like Ed's family. That was good for eternity. But what comfort or hope did the Lord provide for the everyday problems of life?

This was something different. I was puzzled. In my growing-up and our early married life it had not been this way. What was wrong?

CHAPTER 3

LIFE BEGINS

I was born in Jacksonville, Florida, but my parents moved to Donelson, Tennessee, when I was four years old. It may have taken the depression of the 1930s longer to have its impact on Donelson than upon the big cities, but by the mid 1930s it sat heavily on the front porches of that little town. This was the place, and these were the circumstances of my earliest remembrances.

Nashville was only 30 miles away, but in those days it seemed like 100 miles. Nashville was a big city, and when you were six years old—if you were good, didn't fight with your brother or tease your sisters—you might be taken there once a year.

Life in Donelson was an adventure for a growing boy. But the pace quickened just before my first school year when Daddy moved us to the outskirts of Nashville to a 10 acre plot of land, big enough to support a garden, chickens, two goats and a cow. This pastoral scene wasn't created by my parents simply to give us the advantages of country living,

27

ala "Green Acres." Rather we *ate* the turnips and corn. And we *milked* the cow to stay alive.

Living was stringent in those days, sort of "close to the belt," but I don't recall suffering from any hardships. And as I look back now, it was a good life from which I benefited much. I'm sure Nick and my sisters Margie and Judy agree.

My father was starting in the construction business in Nashville and he worked long hours. This meant that he plowed and planted the garden. Weeding it and doing the other outdoor chores—including taking care of Rosemary the cow—were left to Nick and me. He and I took turns giving her the "glad hand."

In some ways Rosemary and I were very close. Alone in the barn early in the morning and again at night, I sang a lot and she didn't appear to mind. I confided to her my secret dreams and most cherished ambitions. But Rosemary was also an embarrassment to me, particularly in my teen-age years.

As the years passed, our neighborhood became a somewhat sophisticated suburb, and Rosemary, bless her memory, sometimes wandered out of her pasture. The telephone would ring and a neighbor, in amusement or irritation, depending upon where Rosemary was and what she had left behind, would say, "Mrs. Boone, it's that cow of yours again!"

I came to dread those times when I had to run across the well-manicured lawns of our neighbors, herding Rosemary back to her stall in the barn. I'm afraid I wasn't as gentle to Rosemary at those times as her bovine psyche might have wished!

Another embarrassment to me in those days was Daddy's Chevrolet pickup truck which carried the inscription on its door, "Boone Construction Company." It would have been different if we had to ride in it only on weekdays. But no. Up until I was in the eighth grade this was our only car. On Sundays Nick and I rode on an improvised bleacher seat on the back while Daddy, Mama and the girls occupied the cab when we drove to church. When it rained, you guessed it, all six of us sardined into the front seat!

As we got older, Nick and I persuaded Daddy to slow down a block or so before we arrived so we could hop out and walk to church in a more dignified manner.

My father was a gentle man who rose at 5:30 a.m. to read his Bible an hour before going to work. He was always ready with thoughtful advice and philosophical counsel. Mama was more direct. And since Daddy's contracting business kept him busy all day and many evenings, my sisters, Nick and I came under Mama's more disciplined tutelage most of the time. She kept an old sewing-machine belt hanging on the bathroom door-knob as an "enforcer"!

Each of us had assignments: Nick and I outside, Marjorie, two years younger than I, and Judy, 5 years younger, inside the house. Mama's approach was very practical.

"You know what you're supposed to do. So do it," was her attitude.

And I guess we pretty well did it! When we didn't— we didn't sit down too good!

Mama was not a hard taskmaster. But she was a just one, and she never flinched from the responsibility. When she said we would be punished for a misdemeanor, we were. I think we all respected Mama for her consistency. She was honest; she kept her word.

What's more, as Nick and I grew older Mama was never intimidated by our size. Before she married she had been a registered nurse. Her ability to handle adult men in the hospital came in handy with her growing boys.

Grady Wilson, long-time friend and associate evangelist of Billy Graham, claims his mother kept a razor strap hanging handily in the kitchen. Over it was a card on which she had lettered the words: "I NEED THEE EVERY HOUR."

Well, I don't recall that Mama needed any reminder. Her

old sewing machine belt just seemed to materialize in her hand when needed. . .even at 17 when I received my last flailing!

But discipline was only a small part of life in those days of my childhood. Most of it was spent out of doors in the near-by athletic fields and in the woods. As a direct descendent of the pioneer Daniel Boone, I tried to live up to my heritage. My success, however, was fairly well limited to breaking my nose three times, my right arm, left wrist and a collarbone and all that I ever "bagged" in the woods was poison ivy.

My world was a secure one in those days—both physically and spiritually.

My first recollections on the religious side are of church, in Donelson. As a family we sat on the front row. Although I don't recall ever asking my parents why, I assume it was so that we kids could be where the action was. . .and where we'd have to behave! When I was very young this didn't always work.

Oh no—I remember many times when Mama took me by the hands and marched me out the center aisle during the church service. After I danced a brisk quick-step in a vain effort to avoid severe seat-burn, Mama ushered me right back up front.

Apparently these incidents made an impression on others as well as myself. Many years later I was on a tour when a woman came up to me after the performance. "Are you the Boone boy from Donelson? The one your Mama used to whale the daylights out of at church?" she asked.

But God was real, as well as institutional, in those days.

As a family we prayed at the dinner table; we had devotionals. And as a boy alone in the woods or riding on my bike I thought about God, and talked to Him. Occasionally I went to Him with a specific request.

When I was around 12, I remember visiting the Smiths up the street with my mother. Milford Smith was my best friend, and we spent the afternoon playing catch with a brand new baseball Daddy had brought home from the Nashville Vol's game. I threw a high one which Milford reached for, but not being eight feet tall, couldn't pull down. It sailed out into the tall grass at the back of the lot.

For half an hour we looked for that ball. The thing had disappeared completely!

Then Mama called, "Time to go, Pat."

Feverishly we stomped down the grass looking for the ball. It was new. Daddy had paid good money for it. Stubbornly, I didn't want to leave it. Mama called again. This time she meant business because she added, "Right now!"

Suddenly the thought struck me, "Why not pray?"

I shut my eyes and said, "Please, God, help me find the ball."

I don't recall what my thoughts were at the time, but when I opened my eyes in the deepening dusk I was looking at a faint white spot barely showing in the tall grass. It was the ball!

Many times since then I have thought back to this incident. In the early days of my career, when I was trying to determine what songs I should record or whether I should accept certain parts in motion pictures, I recalled this answer to prayer. Later on the needs became more desperate. When it appeared that my career was going down the drain, my marriage was on the rocks, and the bank was demanding $1,300,000 overnight I asked the question.

"Can God provide answers to complicated problems such as these, as well as to the simple concerns of a 12-year-old boy?"

The answers to that question you'll find in the pages to come.

How did those formative years contribute to the direction my life was to take? I guess you could say I was "eager" and "persistent," but that's about all.

One summer when I was about nine I was so impressed with the mass of buttercups that grew along our fence that I thought somebody might like to have some in his home. I tied them in bunches and persuaded Mama to let me stand on Granny White Pike near our home and hock them. Only trouble was that when people stopped I could never bring myself to name a price.

"Whatever you want to pay," I would say.

Unconsciously, the psychology may have proved to be more effective than I realized. At least some afternoons would net me as much as a dollar.

The following year I had my first taste as a performer. This involved singing for banana splits Saturday afternoon at the Belle Meade Theater "Happiness Club" in Nashville. I auditioned at the Elizabeth Bryant Combs dance studio where seven or eight kids were picked each week to perform at the Saturday matinees. Ex-vaudevillian Ed Jordan managed the theater and ran the talent contest.

The experience was great. The audience yelled and threw popcorn at each other (and the performers) until Jordan threatened to eject them. As I recall, this melee never bothered me. I sang in the barn to Rosemary, and she didn't pay any attention either. I liked to sing and I liked banana splits. So in the midst of the pandemonium I sang for my own enjoyment.

But I had other interests as well. In those days I was a voracious reader of comic books and kept huge stacks of them in my room. Somehow or another I had concluded that in 50 years they would become collectors' items, and that I would make a killing by selling them to a museum. By the time I was 12, I was drawing my own comic strips, and when I got to high school I became cartoonist for the school paper. At that time, and even on into my early days in college, I dallied with the idea of making this hobby my life's work.

Then there was the Boone Construction Company. During the summer all during our high school years, both Nick and I worked with Daddy as carpenters' helpers. It was easy to see that Daddy was sort of hoping that one or both of us would like construction work and stay with him. We sampled pouring concrete, toting lumber and digging ditches. It didn't take me long to conclude that construction was not my cup of tea.

A big part of my life was centered around the church. Outside of their family, the church and its activities were central to Daddy and Mama. Both carried responsibilities in the local Church of Christ, and because both attended all of its regular services, we kids were there everytime the doors opened.

This meant that from the early days I was taught Bible stories at home and in Sunday School. All of us participated in the young people's activities of the church. But the Bible was not something we simply learned or studied; its precepts became the way of life for us. The Bible said that God loved us and that we were to love one another. When we didn't, we "sinned" and we were punished for it.

Likewise, God expected us to tell the truth, not to cheat, or steal. Ethics were very simple; right was right, and wrong was wrong.

I mention this here because, as you will discover, not too many years later, I became confused. When the blacks and whites merged and became gray, I didn't know what to do.

Although I may have balked a little, the hours I spent alone in the barn milking Rosemary were good for me. They gave me time to reflect.

"What was life really all about?"

"When I grew up, would I marry and have children? Would I be involved in construction work like Daddy, or was there something else I might do?"

As I recall it, these thoughts crowded my mind a good bit in my twelveth and thirteenth years. Usually they came during those quiet hours while I milked Rosemary. The crisis came one evening when I was alone in the barn. My younger brother Nick had committed his life to Christ and was added to the church the year before. Instead of serving as an incentive, his action actually retarded a similar decision on my part. I didn't want to be sandbagged into doing something simply because Nick had done it. Maybe I was stubborn.

33

But the more I thought about it, the more important it appeared to me that my decision be based on a personal conviction on my part.

That evening I tried to sort out my true feelings.

I liked the way Daddy and Mama lived, and the relationship we had together as a family. This was a happy way of life, and it looked good to me.

The Bible, so far in my life, had provided answers to all of the problems I had faced. There might be some bigger problems in the future that I hadn't yet faced, but I was sure that the Bible could provide the solutions to them as well.

Jesus Christ was very real to me. What He did and said not only solved the problems of the people of His day, but also made sense to me in mine.

Who was I? Where did I come from? Why was I born? Where was I going? These questions were too big for me. My world might be little, but since Jesus had provided the necessary answers so far, I decided that night that I would commit my life and those imponderable questions to Him. Surely if bigger problems came later He would give me the answers to them as well.

So I was baptized as a repentant sinner and confessing believer shortly before my 13th birthday.

In my high school days I guess you would have to call me impulsive. Too often I acted before thinking. One glaring example of what I mean has been an embarrassment to me ever since. In fact, if I did not sincerely believe that God forgives us when we confess our mistakes and restores us into a right relationship with him, it may be that my foolishness in this instance might have scarred my future life indelibly.

How it all started, I don't remember exactly. All I know is that a high school buddy of mine and I began to pick up items off the counters of the downtown Nashville stores. It started with small and seemingly insignificant things. Soon, however, we had branched off into neckties, sweaters,

34

compacts, scarfs, etc. It was Christmas time, and we used our pilfered items as Christmas gifts to our friends.

How I justified this activity, for the life of me now, I do not understand. I was a Christian; I wanted to live for God, yet here I was involved in shoplifting.

But God is faithful to those who have committed themselves to Him. Like King David of old, who acknowledged his sin and confessed it before God and was forgiven by Him, I knew I had to do the same.

I went to Mack Craig the principal and told him what I had done. Then I got a job on Saturdays to earn enough money to pay the store owners the retail price for the merchandise I had stolen.

For the next few months, Mack Craig would go to one store after another with the money and tell the store owner what had happened. They were astonished, of course, because they expected a certain amount of this, but didn't anticipate anyone feeling guilty enough to do anything about it.

I can only say that when we acknowledge Him in our lives, God keeps our consciences sensitive enough so that when we do sin, we recognize it. And because of our love for God, we can acknowledge the sin and turn from it.

Another very important lesson emerged during my high school years. Like most boys, I began high school with the ambition to succeed in athletics. By then I was almost six feet tall and had begun to fill out. As a result I played varsity baseball, basketball and tennis.

Meanwhile, however, I had also determined that I ought to become involved in the political activities of the student body. So I asked the Lord to show me how I could make the best possible contribution. Somewhat to my surprise, He answered this prayer quickly by allowing me to be elected president of the freshman class. Later, I was also elected Junior class president.

"This is good," I thought. "But if the Lord has given me

this, maybe I should ask him for the opportunity of becoming student body president when I became a Senior. After all, that would be the top honor, with opportunity in a school career!"

Again I prayed, and determined to prepare myself as best as I could for the position. I even volunteered for tough, unwanted jobs because I thought the experience would help me. At the same time I kept my grades up and usually was right around the top of the class.

Then a strange thing happened. In my junior year a guy came into our class who was transferred from a reform school. He was a great athlete and soon captured the imagination of the student body. When the time came for election for the student body president he was nominated, as was I.

In the campaign that followed I really worked on my speeches, attempting to offer constructive suggestions and ideas. But Russ, who had had no experience and whose primary interest was athletics, goofed his way through his talks. The freshmen and sophomores loved it, though, and to my shock and chagrin I was defeated! Russ became the student body president.

"Why Lord?" I couldn't help but ask. "I prepared for this position, and then prayed that You would show me how to make my testimony for Jesus Christ count in it. Now a fellow who has made a mockery of the office has been elected. How come?"

But I was talking so fast and complaining so bitterly, I couldn't hear His answer. After a couple of days had passed I began to listen to Him. After all, I had prepared myself for this responsibility—and Russ had not. It was only right, then, that I should offer my experience to him, and if he wished to take advantage of it, maybe the Lord could use me in a secondary position.

So I went to Russ and offered to help.

"You're going to be busy with basketball and baseball,

36

Russ," I told him, "and if I can be of any help to you in back-stopping you on the student council or anywhere else, I'll be glad to."

He said he appreciated it and would definitely call on me. He knew he needed the help, and was grateful I had offered it.

Then curiously, that summer Russ married and thereby became ineligible to hold office as student body president. When we returned to school in the fall another election was held, and I was elected.

The lesson was a good one for me. When I was willing to humble myself, because I believed God had called me to do a certain job, He let me learn my lesson, and then gave me back the opportunity which I thought I had lost.

CHAPTER 4

BIRTH OF THE CAREER

I sang for milk shakes at the Belle Meade Theater into my 13th year. The next year I lost my amateur standing when a man gave me $5 to sing some western and pop numbers at a Kiwanis club dinner. By now my appetite plainly was whetted. I sang for the Lions, the Kiwanis or anybody who was willing to pay me a few dollars or give me a free meal. Every contest that came to town I entered—and lost. But losing didn't matter to me. Not yet, at least.

When Horace Heidt and his band arrived in Nashville one year they sponsored a contest in which the winner would be given the opportunity of going on the road with them. Of course I entered; this time Mama objected.

"But why do you want to enter that contest?" she asked.

"It's fun to sing," I responded. "And besides, I might win."

"But if you win, do you think we're letting you leave home and school and go with that band?" she remonstrated.

I hadn't thought of that. But I lost anyway, so it didn't make any difference.

Suddenly, I was offered a bonafide job with a local band. The offer so surprised me I didn't know what to do.

By this time I was attending David Lipscomb High School, a private religious school associated with the Church of Christ. The principal was Mack Craig, a really great guy who loved kids. Through the years since then, Mack has been a warm personal friend and a valued counselor in many sticky situations. I went to him then for advice.

I already had some uneasy reservations about accepting the offer. It would mean late hours, singing at dances which my parents didn't approve of, and being a part of the whole "drinking scene." I suppose I half hoped Mack would say it was all right. But he didn't, and I was relieved when the pressure was off.

But Mack sensed my desire to sing. So he went to work and helped me land my first radio show. It was called "Youth on Parade," and was aired on station WSIX owned by Lewis Draughon. I learned a lot from the program director, Jim McKinney, but "Youth on Parade" had no budget. I served as emcee, host and resident singer my last year in high school and first year in college. Then to my great astonishment—I won my first contest!

I was in my freshman year at Lipscomb College, when I routinely entered a city-wide fund raising affair. Known as the East Nashville Hi Talent Contest, it provided as first prize a trip to New York and an audition for Ted Mack's Amateur Hour on TV.

Frankly, I was more stunned at my good fortune than encouraged to start planning on a singing career. I went on to win the Ted Mack Amateur Hour three times, qualifying for the finals the next summer. I decided right then that winning was more fun than losing! Meanwhile, however, back at college I laid out my curriculum to prepare me for the teaching profession.

The 19th year of my life was a big one for me in another way as well.

In my junior year at high school a new girl had enrolled at David Lipscomb to live in the dormitory while her mother underwent surgery. Because her father was Red Foley, the all-time great country and western TV singer, her reputation preceded her. Most of the guys were more than a little interested. Me too.

That Christmas a heavy snow storm closed all schools in the Nashville area for several days. In the hilarity of the occasion Shirley and I somehow became paired off. We hiked through the snow, skinned down the hills on improvised toboggans—and discovered that we had a wonderful time together.

Meanwhile, Shirley's mother grew increasingly ill, and within a year died. In her grief and lonesomeness Shirley turned to me, and we began to talk about marriage.

For the second time in my life I began to ask myself some serious questions. "Why did I want to marry? What did I expect of the woman I married? What did I intend to offer the girl I married?"

I was attracted by Shirley's gaiety, although she certainly wasn't frivolous. She had a fresh, healthy beauty, like an Olympic swimmer. I was a pretty fair athlete but she could beat me at swimming and table tennis. She was intelligent, a good companion, and above all she lived the way she thought God wanted her to. She was my kind of gal.

Naturally, our parents sensed our seriousness about one another, and expressed their concern. They advised us to slow down, "cool off." My folks wanted me to finish college. Shirley and I felt the same way. But a number of events combined to speed up the timetable.

Red Foley had married again, and Shirley felt somewhat out of place in the new household. She leaned more and more upon me. About this time I began to realize that I had become of age. At 19, legally, I was responsible for making my own decisions.

At my parents request, we tried not to see one another.

41

Their theory was that this would slow down the romance and enable me to finish college before we were married. It had the opposite effect. When we tried dating others, we discovered we were faking. The final blow came when Red Foley announced that he was going to move his family to Springfield, Missouri.

So we eloped on a beautiful fall afternoon in 1953 and were married in Springfield, Tennessee. We took a small apartment near the college, and I got a job in the control room at radio station WSIX. Still, God was with us.

One of the first indications came when I went to Draughon, owner of the radio station WSIX where I had been working on a program without compensation. I told him I was married and that I needed to have a paying job. Immediately he gave me one which, to us, was evidence of the Lord's willingness to bless us for the commitment we had made of our lives to Him, and to each other.

With my job and both of us on a regular classroom schedule, we saw each other practically "by appointment"! And because I could see that there was a danger we would lean too much on our parents in this situation, in January of the next year we took off for Denton, Texas, where I enrolled in North Texas State Teachers College.

The events that followed during our time in Texas were great experiences on which to draw in later years. I've often thought: "If God had not been so real to us then, would we ever have been able to weather the tumultuous years that followed in Hollywood when our faith almost disappeared?"

Although we were young (and maybe a little headstrong), I'm convinced that our decision to elope was also an act of faith. I don't regret what we did, but neither do I recommend it for our own daughters or for anyone else, for that matter. Too great a risk is involved. Fifty per cent of today's teen marriages end in divorce.

God taught us some good lessons of faith in our first year and a half of married life in Texas. Not only did we learn how to trust Him for our financial needs (we *had* to!), but I also recall one occasion when He clearly answered prayer along another line.

I had taken the assignment of preaching in a little country church at Slidell. All the folks there were older than I, a fact that gave me the old sweaty palms syndrome.

"They probably know a lot more about the Bible than I do," I thought. "They think I'm just a college kid—and I am."

But somehow, I believed God would help me, since I was all the preacher they had. There were times when they had precious little, too, but I managed to hang on.

One day one of the elders came to me after the service. "There is a family out our way we've been trying to get interested in church. We've tried everything but they just won't come. They need to know Jesus Christ, and we'd like to have you visit them."

"Sure, I'll be glad to," I responded.

Later in the week I headed out for Slidell to make my call. I was almost there when suddenly the thought struck me.

"What am I going to say?"

I realized again that I was only a college kid. These were adults, hard working farmers, no doubt with a large family. They'd probably laugh at me.

Again I realized, as I had on a few other occasions in my life when I was up against an impossible situation, that no matter how difficult the problem might be, God did have the answer. In my moment of desperation I slammed on the brakes and pulled over to the side of the road. As simply and plainly as I knew how, I told God that I had given my life to Him, and that I wanted Him to use it as effectively as possible. Then I told Him I wanted to be of help to this farm family. I asked Him to show me how and help me not be afraid.

By the time I reached the farmhouse I was perfectly relaxed. And we began the conversation easily. We talked about the weather, crops—and then, quite naturally, about the church and my desire to have them attend our worship service. They readily agreed to, and did!

It was an exhilarating, faith-building experience; God was there—He heard me! He answered my prayer! It was like the lost baseball, the student body election, the talent contest, the first paying job. When I cried out to Him, when I needed Him and knew it, He was listening. He answered!

We took this life of faith up to New York City a year and a half later. I had won the Ted Mack Amateur Hour three consecutive weeks in 1953; in the summer of 1954 I went from Denton to New York and appeared on the Ted Mack finals, but was disqualified for also winning the Arthur Godfrey Talent Scouts the same week! It was an exciting week, but when it ended, I'd gone back to school at NTSC.

However, in 1955 I recorded two gold records, "Two Hearts" and "Ain't That a Shame", both of which sold over a million each. And in the summer of 1955 Godfrey invited me back to appear on his show several times. At the end of the last "guest shot," his parting words were, "Any time you're in New York, Pat, my boy, I want you on the show. I mean any time; just drop in. . . ."

With these words still ringing in my ears, and after two exciting summers in New York City, the prospect of spending two more years in Denton in order to graduate from NTSC seemed unrealistic—my foot was in the door. Shouldn't I barge on in? Shirley and I talked about it—and prayed.

Since the Lord didn't seem to have any objections, at least that we could see, we decided this was it. It didn't take us long to pack and get on our way to New York City. I enrolled at Columbia University, and then walked into Arthur Godfrey's office.

"You said any time I was in New York I could appear on your show, so here I am," I said. The ol' redhead chuckled, and I became a regular part of his show. This was the be-

44

ginning of an exciting five years—the end of one era and the beginning of another.

The era that began to close was the period of great faith in God, and at least a degree of commitment to Him. Up to this time we had almost nothing, and had learned to trust Him to provide for our needs. Our faith was real but it was young, and probably because it did not grow, it soon began to taper off.

This is where the beginning of the new era began. Before I left New York I recorded 10 more gold records with over a million sales each. Some were: "Anastasia", "Love Letters in the Sand", "Friendly Persuasion", "April Love" and "Wonderful Time Up There."

These, plus my appearances on the Arthur Godfrey show, other TV shows and concert dates, gave me increased confidence I was a performer in my own right, and slowly it seemed I didn't have to trust the Lord as I had in the past.

We were active in the Manhattan Church of Christ, which in those days met in a brownstone house at East 80th and Madison Avenue. It was a small and struggling group, but perhaps because our facilities were poor, our faith was great. We were all very close and we had an impossible job to do.

During the six years that Shirley and I participated in the activities of the church, everybody worked hard to raise a million dollars necessary to build an attractive church building. All of us labored thousands of hours on the project. We often invited our friends from the entertainment industry to join us in our little worship services and Bible studies. They came and were impressed by our enthusiasm and convictions, but above all by our concern for the Spiritual welfare of people.

"You really care for people," they would tell us. And our answer was "After all, the church is not the building—it's the people!"

I thought of this recently when I was in New York filming *The Cross and the Switchblade*. The new church has now been built. It cost $2 million instead of $1 million. It's a magnificent building. But when I visited the church I was shocked to discover that there appeared to be fewer people! The setting was beautiful—but strangely quiet, less personal. In the three months I spent in New York City filming the picture, I attended regularly. I couldn't help but tell some of my old friends,

"You know, before we had this new building we were concerned about people. That's all we had. And others were attracted by our love and intense desire to work with God to accomplish an "impossible" task. And He answered our prayers! But now that the new church building is a reality, maybe we've come to depend upon the *building* to attract the people. Maybe that's why we're not growing. Maybe God's reminding us that the church is not the building— *it's the people."*

Despite the happy influence of the church, however, in the late 1950s I was more and more taken up with my career. Its involvements were new and different. The new friends I made also were different; their objectives in life were not the same as mine. Whereas God had been an all important factor in my personal life and in our considerations as a family, to them He was virtually nonexistent. At least they acted as though there were no God.

Shirley was busy at home having babies, so she wasn't so aware of this as I was. And since these people became increasingly important to the success of my career, I became one sort of person to them, while I tried to remain the old Pat Boone to my wife Shirley.

By this time the "Pat Boone image" had begun to develop. I was the nice clean all-American boy who lived next door and wore white buck shoes. That was the kind of song I sang. And as the opportunity to do motion pictures came along, this was the image I portrayed in films.

The first was *Bernadine.* It was the story of a bunch of Boone-type kids, their pranks and mishaps, their romantic involvements, music and "growing pains."

The second was *April Love*. The story here cast me as a semi-delinquent who was transformed into a Boone-type kid on a farm in Kentucky. Shirley Jones taught me to ride a horse.

The last film I made while still in New York was *Mardi Gras,* in which I played a Boone-type kid who happened to be a military cadet at VMI. I was rapidly becoming known as a Boone-type kid!

By this time we had decided to move to California. In 1960 I was well along into the second era of my spiritual life. Had I known then what the future would hold in the next five years, I might have melted down the gold records and quit while I was ahead!

CHAPTER 5

ON THE WAY DOWN

Shirley and I purposely left Tennessee, to be away from both our families and to be on our own. We felt that too many young people get married and play house. They live in the parents' home of one or the other, and don't have any responsibilities. Well, we had plenty. We were living by faith and $44.50 a week! Sundays I preached in a little country church. Even though we didn't have much, we were very close and utterly dependent upon each other.

When we first moved I didn't have a job. But I thought, with the credentials I had from experience in television and radio in Nashville, and with papers of recommendation from managers or owners of the stations, it wouldn't be too difficult to find a job somewhere.

But no, I struck out completely. They didn't need me. They still laugh about it at the one big station in Dallas, WFAA. They were looking for a singer, but after the audition they weren't interested.

"What's the matter?" I asked.

"Your voice is too soft," they replied.

I was eager and hungry, "But I can sing louder. . . ."

Nonetheless, they turned me down cold. And no job was in sight. Then I was offered a chance to sing for good money with a dance band, like before in Nashville. The temptation was great because our money was running out, and by now Shirley was expecting our first child.

Yet I couldn't conscientiously take that job singing with the dance band. So we felt surely God would provide something else. By now I was looking for any kind of work I could get!

The fellow living below us in our apartment house had a wonderful job. He drove a big car, and all he did was to get up early in the morning and spend a couple of hours delivering newspapers. So I thought I would try a paper route. I went to the manager of the circulation department at the *Fort Worth Star Telegram.* He laughed.

"Man, you don't just walk in and get a paper route. You have to *inherit* these things!"

We talked a little bit, and I told him I had come to Fort Worth originally for a singing job.

"Have you been over to WBAP in Fort Worth, the station the *Star Telegram* owns?" he asked.

I told him I hadn't. That was the one station I had not gone to because it was the biggest in the whole area. I didn't tell him I had figured that if I couldn't get a job at the smaller stations I certainly had no hope of getting one in the largest in the whole Southwest.

The circulation manager wanted to be helpful, thank God. So he called the station manager and made an appointment for me. That appointment got me in.

I was rushed into the manager's office. The program director was there, and they talked with me like I was something special.

"We think we've got a show for you to do. Do you play the guitar?"

50

I said, hesitantly, "No, I play a ukulele."

"That's not important. Why don't you start on our Friday night show?"

So without an audition, and assuming I was a country singer because I came from Tennessee, they put me on the Bewley, a Barn Dance show!

I didn't sing country music and never had. I didn't volunteer that information, though (they didn't ask me). I even had to go out and buy some jeans.

Somewhere along the way I had sung *The Navajo Trail* from a Bing Crosby movie, so I brushed up on that and came in Friday night with some brand-spanking new blue jeans and did my best to look western. I even bowed my legs a little.

But that first afternoon I returned from Fort Worth and trudged slowly up the back steps of our ramshackled apartment building. I walked in with a down-cast expression on my face. Shirley came over put her arms around me. "Don't worry, honey. We'll get along. The Lord will provide somehow," she said.

When I told her I had been offered a job at $50 a week we whooped and hollered and jumped up and down.

I went to work on the barn dance, and within a few weeks became the host of it. They asked me to do a teen-age show. I hosted that and did the commercials, sang the songs, did the interviews. Now our financial problems appeared to be solved.

Then came the opportunity to compete in the Ted Mack Amateur Hour Finals in New York City. While I was there, I also won Arthur Godfrey's Talent Show, and appeared with him for a week.

All of this happened so quickly that sometimes it seemed breath-taking. During this period Shirley trusted me to come up with the right answers. We looked to God for them. Sometimes I would find them in the Bible, other times they came in answer to prayer. As a result I guess she sort of had me

51

on a pedestal.

When we moved to New Jersey the pace quickened. I was going to college fulltime, and our four children were born before I graduated: Cheryl Lynn, first, then Linda Lee, Debora Ann and Laura Gene. Although we did have the normal tensions, pressures and problems that come from a busy schedule, somehow the excitement of recording sessions, the Godfrey show, TV specials and new babies kept us close together.

When we moved to California, I quit my television show to make the film, *Journey to the Center of the Earth.* We decided to concentrate on movies and quit the grind of weekly TV performances. Now I had to go out of town for weeks at a time on a film set or on a concert tour.

Shirley couldn't go because the children were little. What troubled her so much was that she knew my standards were starting to change or slip. For one thing I had begun to drink a bit. Partly because I had been in Europe where it was more normal to drink wine than water. Also, I had been with missionary friends in Germany who said they had to drink beer with the people in order to reach them with the Gospel. I claimed this as a basis for my feeling that there wasn't anything inherently wrong with alcoholic beverages.

So gradually, when I came home to the U.S. and would go to a Hollywood party or some other glittery clambake where everybody else was drinking, I didn't see any reason for not having something to drink. It obviously was not wrong in itself.

At home we were confronted with the question of dancing for our girls. My position was that we didn't want to warp their personalities by making them too different. And while these may seem like minor matters, my attitude toward them represented a shift in standards that confused and bewildered Shirley.

More and more, where I had always been shy around women, now I found it easy to talk with them. When I had been left in a room with Carmel Quinn, on the Godfrey Show, or with one of the McGuire sisters—even though they were married and I was married—I became uneasy and showed it. I could feel perfectly secure with hundreds or before millions of people, but put me with one woman and I began to choke up. But now Shirley could see I was becoming more at ease around individual women. There had been no jealousy at all in those early years; now a concern began to grow in Shirley because she saw how much I enjoyed these contacts.

Also I was telling jokes that by most any standard were improper or indecent. Obviously I was changing to a greater and greater degree.

She saw that I could move with equal ease from a Hollywood cocktail party to a church pulpit. I appeared to be able to switch from one to the other, lay down one set of standards and pick up another as the occasion demanded it.

She'd confront me with these things. I would agree with her—usually in quiet moments when we'd lie in bed at night.

"Pat, you know we aren't studying the Bible, we're not praying, we're not talking to anybody about the Lord. We're just going along as if we didn't think it was important. . .as if our friends who are not even Christians are just as safe and secure as we are and it doesn't matter to us.

"We've got more money than we need. We have influence. We have the knowledge of the Bible and all the training in the world. . .yet we don't do a thing with it. We just go to church and have our little private devotions. Won't God hold us responsible?"

I had no real answer. So, I would shrug off what she was saying. Away on the road, I would go to a party on Saturday night and be out until two or three in the morning. During those hours I would engage in a lot of ribald, suggestive conversation with many people including young women. I found it easy and enjoyable. An occasional drink, the loud music, and the titilating awareness that some young lovely was obviously "available"—all seemed more and more fun.

53

But the next morning I would be in church and Sunday School. It made me feel good to realize that Pat Boone, the entertainer, who was appearing in town last night, got up and came to church.

Sometimes the minister would acknowledge this from the pulpit, and I liked the sound of what he said. Of course, I hoped no one would smell my breath.

So Shirley would compare the "new" me with the Pat Boone and the family life we used to have; and the picture wasn't good. I didn't like it when she made the comparison, either.

"Look," I said. "We all change. We've got to change. We can't always be naive children just blindly trusting in God. We've got real problems to grapple with, and I guess along the way we have to learn to compromise."

But Shirley had known the time when I had been the true spiritual leader. I made the decisions based on what I believed God wanted, *not on what I thought the situation demanded.* In Hollywood the situation worsened. I spent more and more time at parties and places like the Factory and the Daisy. If Shirley couldn't or wouldn't go, I would go alone. And when I came home she could often tell I had been drinking.

One night it was particularly bad. We were filming a scene in *Good-Bye Charlie* with Debbie Reynolds.

I played a naive "mama's boy" kind of character. I realized at the time it was a caricature of what many people really thought about me — as something of a square and a little naive. In other words, I was playing a part in the movie that was Pat Boone — plus! But I played it all the way — to the extent of drinking champagne and to the point of really getting half-bombed.

The scene took all afternoon and many takes! When I finally got home, foggy, and late for dinner, Shirley felt she was looking at a stranger! Certainly I was no longer the man of high moral standards she had once known me to be.

CHAPTER 6

DOUBLE TROUBLE

I continued to insist that we attend church regularly as a family.

"It's a good habit," I said.

"How can you say that?" Shirley replied. "Why go to church out of habit? If it doesn't mean any more than that, it's not worth anything."

Her reaction irritated me, partly because it threatened my authority as the head of the house. All my life I'd read the Bible. In college I had studied Greek and read from the New Testament in its original language. I had considerable knowledge of church history and doctrine. Now my wife doubted my dedication or leadership—or both! It was tough to swallow.

However, I was able to suppress my feelings. In the first place, I'm not a thin-skinned guy, usually, I can take criticism and shrug it off without feeling hurt. Also, I was willing to admit that there was an element of truth in what she said.

Frankly, I didn't know what to do about it. Some people

were always critical of me—especially church people. I received letters from those who felt I was wrong in even being *in* the entertainment industry!

"How could you have been on that program or have done that dance number?" they asked. Or, "How could you kiss that girl in that movie?"

Gradually I became used to some people thinking I was hypocritical because I didn't meet their standards. Inwardly, of course, I knew I was hypocritical, and that I was not so committed to the Lord as I ought to be or would like to be. But I had gotten to the point where *I was trying to balance the life of an entertainer with that of a Christian.* I reasoned that if I was to be an entertainer, I could not go too far on the one hand into the Lord's camp; and on the other, if I was a Christian, I couldn't plunge "whole hog" into the entertainment business.

I knew I wasn't getting much out of my kind of Christianity; and at the same time I had the feeling that my professional life was suffering too. It was miserable.

Because I was neither fish nor fowl I went through some harrowing experiences.

In 1959 I went to Europe to do a TV special. Shirley went with me. We did two shows in Paris, one in Salzburg and one in Venice. I had already done three films, *Bernadine, April Love* and *Mardi Gras.* All three were successful.

Now Buddy Adler, head of 20th Century Fox, had the lead part for me to play in a film called *The St. Bernard Story.* This was a part he insisted was academy award caliber, but it required me to play a Catholic monk. This clashed with my Protestant Christian beliefs, which intellectually I still clung to. I didn't see how I could put on the robes of a Catholic monk; and yet, professionally, I wanted to.

It was a fine story in which a monk and a young girl fall in love, but deny themselves because of their faith. Shirley and I prayed about it, and we agonized over it. We had talked to preachers before we left the U.S., and to mission-

56

aries we met in Europe. I had asked my manager and agents to see what they could do.

Finally they worked out a statement, and incredibly it was accepted, to appear at the beginning of the film. It was to say, "Mr. Boone wishes to state that as a member of the Church of Christ he does not necessarily endorse all the practices or doctrine depicted in the film, but wants to join with us of 20th Century Fox in thanking the Monks of the St. Bernard Monastery for making this picture possible."

Adler said, "Okay, we'll put this kind of a statement at the beginning of the film. We hate it. We think it's from the dark ages, but we'll go ahead with it."

Even then, I wasn't sure. Shirley and I were staying in the Grand Hotel in Venice on this particular occasion. We had invited some missionaries and ministers up to our room. We were on our knees praying together that God would help us know what my final decision should be. It was beyond me. I didn't think *I* could come up with the right answer, so I wanted these spiritual men to pray with me. I thought somehow they might get through if I couldn't.

While we were praying the phone rang. We tried to ignore it, but it kept ringing. Finally I got up to answer it.

It turned out to be a long distance call from Nashville from Mack Craig, my former high school principal. He had been my spiritual advisor and close friend since those days.

Back then he had given me a little slogan to help in making decisions. It was simple and I had used it often: in the final analysis, strip away everything else, and ask "Is it *right* in itself?" Not what you want, or is easiest, or the good you think could come from it. But "is it right?"

Mack said, "I've been praying about this movie, and I think you would be wrong to do it. It might be fine for someone else, but not for you."

That settled it. Here we had been praying in Venice for an answer to this dilemma, and a long distance call comes right then all the way from Nashville. What other indication did I need?

57

So I called Buddy Adler in Los Angeles that night. *He hit the ceiling!* He threatened to suspend me for non-performance of contract.

"You know, if we suspend you, this will mean you'll be through! No more recordings, because the musicians' union will go along with us. No television either," he said.

I realized what a tough position he was in. It just didn't make sense to him. It appeared too bigoted and narrow.

I said, "Buddy, I understand how you feel, but it's a matter of conscience with me. I cannot do it, and I hope you won't take these measures you're talking about. But if you want to suspend me — okay. I just cannot do it."

What neither of us knew was that, as we talked on the phone, Adler was dying of cancer. Not long after he had to retire from the studio, and his health failed rapidly.

Then a new studio head came in at 20th and wanted me to do a science fiction picture, a Jules Verne story called *Journey to the Center of the Earth* with James Mason, Arlene Dahl and Diane Baker.

I didn't want to do it. I considered myself a singer; I wanted to do some musical pictures. But they made me a tremendous deal, and it turned out to be their biggest grossing picture of the year!

As a matter of fact, many people believe that it was this film which kept 20th Century Fox alive during the period of its disasterous production of *Cleopatra*. Actually, *Cleopatra* was so expensive that interest payments on loans at one point amounted to $10,000 a day. But the receipts on *Journey to the Center of the Earth* continued to mount. Soon, the studio reps came to me because my royalties on *Journey* had passed what they could afford to pay! They wanted to talk "new deal." In the end, my agent was able to re-negotiate a new contract which proved to be the best I had ever had. In addition to a firmer contract with larger percentages, now I had the opportunity to co-produce additional films! While this was good so far as my career was concerned, yet I can see now that it gave me a false sense of security. I actually began to believe that God *needed* me in the entertainment professions and that was the reason He had given me such opportunities.

This was easy to justify. There were many people in the entertainment profession who either ignored God or who identified with Him only slightly. When I compared myself with them I came out way ahead.

As I looked around, there appeared to be many people in the church who took the same attitude. They compared themselves with people outside the church, and by contrast they looked good! They honestly believed that God *needed* them as churchmembers, teachers in the Sunday School and singers in the choir. They waved the flag for the church and for Christ—whenever they were in church circles. But outside the church they, like I now knew myself to be, were compromisers. They put their personal interests first instead of God.

As I look back, I can see how the Lord was with me in these struggles. I did not put Him first in my life; obviously, my career was number one. But in a way I did try to do what I thought was right. My concern for my career often led to compromises, but somehow the Lord brought me through.

The debilitating thing about compromises, of course, is that one leads to another. Take the matter of smoking, which even before cancer statistics, was of great concern to church people.

Shirley was thinking about smoking to keep her weight down after our first child was born. Both her mother and father smoked, and it was okay with them for her to smoke even while she was a teen-ager at home, although she didn't do it. So it wasn't a matter of a moral issue with her. But I had been brought up in a traditional Christian home where smoking *was* a moral issue. Partly because of this, and partly because I had to prepare talks for my speech class in college,

I developed a powerful dissertation on the damages to health from smoking.

I practiced my talk at the apartment and used the same arguments on Shirley, but they had no effect. What did influence her was my personal appeal:

"Honey, when you smoke cigarettes, you're just not the girl I married. I married a girl with a clean, sweet breath, and wholesome habits. Although I can't think it is a sin for you to smoke, except as it harms your body.

When the shoe was on the other foot, though, it didn't fit so well. As a student at Columbia I got very little sleep. What with TV appearances, recording sessions and film productions, when I hit the classroom for a two-hour lecture I was "gone" in five minutes. I tried eating sandwiches, bringing candy. I actually rubbed salt in my eyes, stuck my leg with a pen knife. Nothing worked.

So finally I started smoking a pipe or a cigar since we were allowed to do it in classes at Columbia, I did the same at home studying.

When I continued after graduating, *Shirley* objected. And she fed my own arguments back to me. They bounced off.

"Look, I enjoy it. I know my speech about nicotine and all that, but I don't inhale and only smoke two pipefuls a day. That's all."

The thing that really ate at me, though, was when she used my own painful "Jekyl and Hyde" approach back on me! "You're just different, Pat—when you smoke, you're just not the guy I married."

Increasingly there was the specter of the compromises I was making as a Christian in the entertainment profession. In his column, Earl Wilson quoted my answer to the question: "Can a person be a Christian and be an entertainer?"

"Yes," I said, "but if ever I reach a point where I believe that being an entertainer is hampering my life as a Christian or that I am not really serving God as a singer, I'll give up the entertainment career."

I would also say the same thing in church services, before Sunday School classes and young people's gatherings. It sounded real good to me at the time. And I think I meant it—at least *one* of me did! But the "other me" was starting to demand equal time. Shirley and I began to drift apart.

It became increasingly difficult for us to communicate with one another. I was going to parties that she just wouldn't go to. And usually she was uncomfortable when she *did* come along.

Once we went to a big opening night at the CopaCabana in New York for a well-known entertaining team that we knew—they'd been on my television show. We sat up front with a big table of friends. The acts were suggestive and the dialogue crude. Everybody at our table was laughing—except Shirley. She sat very quietly, not attracting attention, but ill. She could not pretend to laugh at stuff that she saw as dirty, offensive and certainly un-Christian. And it was, of course. Toward the end of the act there was a standing ovation, but Shirley didn't get up.

This sort of thing ate at me, inside. I thought she was making an unnecessary public spectacle. Shouldn't you go along with what everybody else was doing, even if you didn't wholeheartedly agree with it, so at least you could be polite? I thought so. I didn't censure Shirley for her feelings; she had the right to do whatever she wanted to do. But situations like this were a sign we were growing quite a world apart.

On her part, Shirley was fighting for what she thought was the existence of her family. Parties became the source of many arguments. This represented friction that we had never dreamed would enter into our marriage relationship. We prayed about the matter, Shirley much more frequently than I, but there didn't appear to be an answer. It seemed to me that she was trying to cling to earlier family relationships, and even the children, as a sort of security blanket.

61

We occasionally tried to talk to our minister and some close friends, but they could give us little help. They would rarely go out on a limb and advise us about what we should or shouldn't do. They felt that God had given us a position of influence, and we should use that influence for good. They had varying opinions on stands we should take, but they all sounded somewhat hazy.

Of course, I thought that Shirley was just having trouble adjusting to the requirements of a career life. I said, "Honey, if I were a *preacher,* you'd still have these conflicts and problems. You'd still think I was wrong about a lot of things. You would disagree, and we would still have our personal conflicts. Our lives would be very little different—except that we wouldn't be able to give our kids the things we want to give them, and we would be living a hand-to-mouth existence. Our sphere of influence would also be limited. Here, God has put us in a position of influence. We can't walk away from it. Sure, we've got tough decisions to make. We don't know all the answers, but it won't solve anything for me just to cease to be an entertainer! We'd still be the same two people."

But my talk didn't help. Our marriage was getting shaky. I was increasingly at ease away from home and away from Shirley, and with other people whose ideas and whole manner of life were totally different. She felt like a stick in the mud sometimes because I could come home on Saturday from a busy day, change clothes, have a quick dinner and whizz off to a party. I would come in at one or two o'clock in the morning, then be ready for church!

Meanwhile, Shirley developed an inner physical problem compounded by the emotional crisis that brought it about. I couldn't hold her hand or kiss her without her literally getting nauseous. She was deathly afraid of going to the doctor since she thought he might find something seriously wrong. Whenever I put my arms around her, I could tell she was flinching, setting herself to endure it.

Then I would say to myself, "If that's the way you feel, if that's all I mean to you, well, who needs it?"

She would go to bed, and I'd go down stairs and listen to music until the wee hours of the morning or read awhile and then go to sleep on the couch. . .Until one night I got up, got dressed.

"Where are you going?" Shirley asked.

"I've had all I can take. I'm leaving," I said.

"Is that all your family means to you?"

"Well, you don't care about me. We don't have anything in common any more. What's the use of making believe?" I stormed, pulling on a sweater.

By this time Shirley was out of bed.

"Don't go. I love you, Pat. I don't know what is the matter. . .but this is not the way."

I hesitated, confused and loving my wife, but also feeling bitter and sorry for myself.

Shirley dropped to the floor and held me around the knees.

"If we let God take over, I'm sure He'll help us," she sobbed. "Stay, Pat, please, I don't want you to leave."

We were in a turmoil. The next day Shirley went to the doctor, and he found she had an ovary malfunction which he could and did correct. This gave me some tolerance, but our problems were far from solved.

CHAPTER 7

HOW FAR CAN YOU GO

You can imagine what it would do to a husband, over a three or four month period, when he saw that his very touch would make his wife sick! Everywhere else, people were warm, receptive and even excited by my presence. I enjoyed that. As a result, I wound up not minding being gone from home for longer periods of time.

"Other women think I'm witty; they think I'm attractive, and I get a kick out of their flattering attention. At home with Shirley there's nothing but conflict," I reasoned.

At the same time I had the gnawing suspicion that a lot of conflict came because I did not have the answers I should have had. Should Shirley and I, and the kids, simply adjust to a life of compromise? Was this the inevitable, ultimate answer? Reluctantly, furtively, I toyed with the idea that I might have to give up being an entertainer. We might go back to Tennessee. But. . .if I were to become a preacher or teacher. . .I could still see our home life no different! In other words, I just didn't have any hope that God could solve our problems for us.

About this time I made my first trip to Las Vegas in spite of Shirley's misgivings. Again I could see nothing wrong in it; man, this is Show Biz City! My career demanded it; all the big performers appear there, and that was where I should go!

Yet, I'll never forget the morning when I woke up to realize that the last thing I had done the night before was to write a check for $2,500 — to pay a gambling debt. I felt sick, remorseful and disgusted with myself. But like a lot of other people who go to Vegas, the remorse wore off.

Shirley was particularly disturbed about Las Vegas and pleaded with me to stop going. At various times she'd talk to her friends and to our preacher about the situation. But their response generally, was to counsel her to go along with me. Many of our best friends saw no problem at all.

"It's nice that you go to church and have a good family life," they would say. "But your husband needs you, and if he asks you to sit down and take a glass of wine with him, do it!"

When she hesitated at this advice, they shrugged their shoulders. The result was that she began to wonder whether or not *she* was wrong. It was one thing to be considered a square by some people, and at the same time be appreciated by others. But when both her husband *and* her friends gave her the impression that she was wrong, then she began to question herself.

In this hopscotch kind of existence that we went through for some years during the early 1960's, the husband of one of Shirley's sisters worked for me. At the office we would laugh and kid around about all kinds of things which I feel badly about today. I was going through a period of what I called "liberation" or "freedom." Out on the road with Henry I felt as though I could be somebody different than what I was at home with Shirley and the girls. In a hotel room, at a party, or among intimate friends I was one thing; at church I was something altogether different.

66

Shirley was concerned about her sisters who weren't going to church at this point and who didn't feel any particular need to be close to God. She would say, "Let's study the Bible with Julie or Jenny and their husbands, because they need God just like we do."

When we did, however, Julie's husband would look at me strangely. I would feel uneasy because I knew he had seen me in my show business environment, and it didn't jive with this little group in his home studying the Bible and talking about doctrinal differences between Baptist and the Church of Christ. There was such a conflict between what I believe doctrinally and what Henry saw me practice that I don't wonder he was confused. I was quite firm about both; I would justify both. We talked about such subjects as whether you baptized *for* the remission of sins or *because* of the remission of sins. I was the one who knew the Bible and all the arguments. We talked about instrumental music, and why we didn't think we should have instumental music. It's a tenuous dogma, but I still had all the arguments for it.

They knew that Shirley was deeply spiritual, and they knew she was in earnest. But I'm sure when they looked at me they said, "He may be serious about this, but his life doesn't seem much different than ours. It looks like he's trying to sell us a bunch of strict rules." So they rejected them.

They liked to go out boating on Sundays. They didn't see how they were different *not* going to church, than we were *going* to church. So our Bible studies petered out. Meanwhile, they sensed that all the sailing wasn't smooth with the Boones! So they began to counsel Shirley.

"You've got to relax. You've got to live a little bit. You and Pat are so different in what you think and about how to live. You ought to travel with him on the road."

Other people were saying to Shirley, "Don't let that guy go out on the road without you. Go to the parties with him.

Be with him, because you're not going to keep him—unless you keep him company! Look, Pat may be better than average, but he's still a human being, and there are a lot of gals out there."

Shirley had never doubted my faithfulness before. But now the doubts began to creep in.

I had to admit things were tempting me that never really tempted me before. I used to say I had a "guard-all shield" around me, and my public image was actually a protection for me. Women, I thought, would never make any direct overtures to me because of the way I looked and what they heard about me. But I discovered that when they saw me with a drink in my hand, laughing and enjoying all the things that were going on, that there was a difference. Not only was the "guard-all shield" disappearing, but I felt that was fine.

"If I am going to be part of this entertainment community, they can't think of me as a square. I've got to show that I fit right in. People know that I'm an outspoken Christian. And this is a good lesson: that I can mix right in and be utterly at home at a Hollywood party—do practically anything everybody else does—and still be a Christian," I rationalized.

Of course, I had begun to have inner doubts by this time, "Who do you think you're fooling, Boone? Yourself, maybe?" I asked myself.

For one thing, Shirley was asking deep spiritual questions regarding our relationship to God and His Son, Jesus. My rationalizing wouldn't quite hold water; where once I'd been able to justify my positions, now she was coming up with Scripture (which I knew, but wanted to forget) that poked holes in my arguments.

For another thing, I was beginning to pray—"Lord, have mercy on me;" I know I'm a sinner.

This I prayed sometimes after a long, loud night of parties when I had done or said things that I was ashamed of and knew were wrong. I realized God knew, too—and the thought made me sad. Not scared—sad. We'd been good friends once. Deep in my soul, I missed Him.

Somewhere in that "liberated" period, I felt my lifelong faith in the inspiration of the Bible, in miracles, in God-man relationships begin to slip, to crack. My doubts were being fed and fueled by a desire to broaden my career image—to update it to the swinging type of personality that I thought a successful career required. Dean Martin, Steve McQueen, the Beatles—they were "in." The cleancut type of character that I once had been was now passe. The public, according to Hollywood barometers at least, had changed its view of what a hero should be. And if I was to cut my piece of the pie, I had to "broaden" my personality accordingly.

Around this time I wrote a book entitled *The Care and Feeding of Parents.* It represents a picture of tranquil, happy family life, and appears to say that we had all the answers.

Well, to put it bluntly—it was a fake. It wasn't that I told untruths; the answers I gave were good ones; it was simply that I gave only the *good* side and not the haunting failures and frustrations that dogged me day and night. It was like an old western movie set where the front of the bank building gives the appearance of a thriving place of business. But if you walk through the front door you discover that the whole front is simply propped up by two-by-fours. Inside the door you find grass and weeds instead of a bank.

CHAPTER 8

THIS IS THE END

Somewhere along this twisting, bumpy, downhill road, I accepted the idea that the Pat Boone image should be "adapted" to keep up with the times. I became more convinced when Ray Stark, the producer, offered to buy the remainder of my contract from 20th Century Fox. It called for two films, for a little over $500,000. He was eager to do it because he thought that there would be tremendous commercial value in pulling a switch and changing the so-called "all-American boy" into a Paul Newman or Steve McQueen. The idea was to show that this boy you thought was naive could be a bare-chested, two-fisted kind of guy. You know, like Roy Rogers becoming Humphrey Bogart.

At first I was swept away by the idea. The deal was made. In the first film I was to play an amoral drifter, living with an older woman in her trailer on a circus lot. I fall in love with Nancy Kwan, a virginal young circus performer. Then I realize for the first time in my life what it is to be loved by somebody and to feel love *for* somebody. Nancy's step-father attempts to rape her, and I commit a murder; we leave the circus together. The high point of the script comes when we have the opportunity to go to bed together—and for the first time in my life I *resist* my own impulses and deny myself something I now want more than anything else in the world! I do this because I know that I'm a murderer and this can never be a continuing relationship. For her, it's marriage; for me, it would be just another affair. I can't do it. Of course, we wound up getting together eventually for the usual happy ending, and I thought the story had a moral point.

So we started filming in England. But half way through, they started to change the script. Now they had the two of us actually going to bed together! The script writer and the producer had decided that no guy in his right mind could be alone in a cabin with a beautiful girl and refuse to jump in bed when she offered herself to him.

I hit the ceiling, and sent a three-page telegram from London to the producer back in Hollywood.

A terse cablegram came back, "Just say your lines. We will write the script."

At this point my dander was up, and I tried to back out of the movie and go home. But my lawyer pointed out that there was nothing in my contract about script approval, and that the producer had spent over a million dollars on the film already. Either I had to do it as they planned, or they could sue me for what they had spent already—and more!

So I had to go ahead and finish the film. I was sick already, but then the publicity came out. The thrust was, "Pat Boone's in trouble with that *Susie Wong* girl." (Nancy Kwan had played the prostitute Suzie Wong.) On top of that the motion picture code board refused to give its seal of approval to the film unless they changed some dialogue and altered one of the scenes.

The producer was ecstatic.

"This is the greatest thing that could have happened! We'll

release the film *without* the seal of approval. . .we'll capitalize on the fact that Pat Boone is in a film that didn't get the motion picture seal of approval. . .Tremendous! So what if its banned in a few places? That'll be great!" he said.

For the first time—I began to see where my compromises were taking me. I didn't want to be a "new Pat Boone" in *that* sense! I realize my whole career was built on the "old" Pat Boone; basically I was still the same sort of man. But I could see that I was letting myself get drawn out into a never-never land where I'd be just another actor, and my Christian witness would be lost. Thank God, people stayed away from the film in droves!

Now Shirley was coming to the spiritual crisis of her life. She discovered she was pregnant; but because of our conflicts, the mixed-up spiritual climate in our home, she prayed that God would take this baby. He did; in her fifth month, she had a miscarriage. For so long, she'd been trying to get me to read the Bible and talk about our spiritual problems and give up the hypocrisy in our lives. But I continued to rationalize.

Finally, it seemed to her that the only way out was to surrender her convictions.

Although she didn't realize it at the time, her family had become her god. She had reached the point where it was more important to her to preserve the family than it was to preserve her faith. I'll never forget the day she came to me.

"Honey," she said, "I'm not going to nag anymore. After all, you're the spiritual leader of this house. I only want you to know that *you're taking five other souls with you wherever you go.*"

It had an almost theatrical ring. Hadn't Greer Garson said this to somebody in a movie scene? Part of my problem was that I could see almost everything in life being portrayed in a film. And still—Shirl's statement came like a solar plexus blow. It made me realize that I *must* come up with some kind of direction for our lives.

What shocked me more was what began to happen *now.*

73

Shirley was thinking, "So there isn't anything wrong with double standards? Then I've got to turn loose and be a part of what Pat does, because if I don't—I might lose him."

Naturally this didn't help. Instead of tensions disappearing, they increased. Before this, Shirley's love for me enabled her to overlook my weaknesses and failures and to put up with my double standards. But now that she had hitched her spiritual wagon and those of our kids to *my* ragged shirt-tail, it was a new ball-game! When she saw me make mistakes and do things based on flimsy rationalization, it really began to eat at her. Now she not only saw the wrong, but she saw me as the *perpetrator* of the wrong; certainly not the spiritual leader of the family.

What was even worse, where she had come to distrust herself and to believe that perhaps her judgments were wrong in criticizing me, now she saw me in an altogether new and different light. And the light wasn't good, because it revealed me for what I really was—a two-faced hypocrite. Before she hadn't known all the things that I was getting into, because she didn't *want* to know, but now as she became a part of the scene, she saw how treacherous it was and how involved I had become in it. Naturally, this further disillusioned her.

Of course, I had always gotten a lot of "love letters" from gushing women. In the past we had both shrugged them off with a laugh. But now they weren't so funny to Shirley—especially when they came from places where I had been and sometimes from girls who intimated they'd fly to meet me "anywhere, anytime."

And there was no way for me to convince Shirley that I was still the same bashful guy that I had been, back in the early days of our marriage. Now she *knew* I wasn't. A real wedge of doubt began to separate us. Shirley wouldn't ask me questions; she'd simply hand me a letter that had come in, and let me read it. While I did, she'd leave.

I didn't think I should start getting defensive and deny

things that Shirley hadn't even accused me of. Yet we both knew that the suspicion was there—and no reason that it shouldn't be, since I was gone from home so much. This put a greater strain than ever on the times we *did* have together.

But now that Shirley had determined to cut loose from her former standards and follow me, the picture changed altogether. Not only did she go with me to parties and premiers, and sometimes travel with me, but she also became a different kind of person. She began to drink occasionally and to mix in with "the beautiful people." This came partly as a result of advice from close friends who were really trying to help—but purely from a human standpoint.

And so—the two of us abandoned her frail vision of light, and hand in hand, we walked into the darkness.

At first this was fine with me; at least we were together, unified. Then we'd be at a party and I'd look over and see some handsome young actor monopolizing Shirley's time and coming on strong; I'd start to see red. Could she be enjoying it? This happened more and more.

Once in Reno an actor friend, who was appearing there the same time I was, got half loaded and confessed how he had made a pass at Shirley when I was gone and how she had resisted him.

But now I was so guilty of my own transgressions that I couldn't really blame him! Instead, I began to be suspicious, for the first time in my life, of what Shirley was doing at home while I was gone.

On top of everything else, now my career was traveling a rocky road. Directors and scriptwriters were no longer interested in my "teen-age Lawrence Welk" image. Although I've never seen myself that way, I realized that in the sophisticated eyes of the entertainment colony, I was not what you'd call a real, all-out "swinger." And who was I kidding? I knew I could *never* be a rebel or a sex symbol like Paul Newman or Steve McQueen. A period of real frustration began. For the first time in some years, I wanted to be what I knew I really was—a straight, rather decent guy. But I couldn't get the pieces back together!

One of the first attempts was making a pilot program for a NBC show with Gene Rodney (he produced *Father Knows Best)*. Gene herded an excellent cast into a warm family story called *My Island Family.* It was about a young engineer on a South Pacific island with a young Peace Corps nurse and a bunch of happy natives.

The pilot turned out great. But. . .it was the year of the *Adams Family, The Munsters* and such "gimmick" shows as *I Dream of Jeannie, Bewitched,* and *The Beverly Hillbillies.* The show was too bland, and nobody bought it.

Strange, the more I tried to do the right thing, the more everything bombed out. I made a couple of other pilots; they looked sensational, but you guessed it: zero. And I was making records of songs that sounded like hits to me, but they wound up in radio station wastebaskets all over America.

For example, I recorded *By the Time I Get To Phoenix.* Everybody could tell it should be a hit. We knew at that time that Glen Campbell, who had only one hit record, was also recording the song; but we had a three-week head start. Great; just then, there was a complete changeover in the Dot record management, and production lagged. Glen Campbell's terrific version came out, and boom: he had a smash hit! Meanwhile, my record never got to Phoenix!

It seemed like I couldn't do anything right. So I began to feel sorry for myself.

"Why God? Isn't it important to decent people that they have a Christian voice in the entertainment world? Doesn't the church need me? Don't you need me. . .? Why won't you do something about my career?" I complained. "I've done everthing *I* know to do—please help me. My marriage, my career, my children—please!"

I was at the bottom—with nowhere to look but up.

76

CHAPTER 9

A GLIMMER OF LIGHT

I searched my soul. And I began to remember some things.

I remembered, with tingling warmth, a wonderful human being named Clinton Davidson. What a joy he was to know — what a happy, fulfilled man!

Clint started out as the "world's *worst* insurance salesman;" it took him five years before he was able to increase his earnings to $200 per month! At that time, most insurance salesmen were able to reach that production in the first year.

Yet a few years later, Clinton Davidson was hailed as the world's *greatest* insurance salesman! For many years his annual volume exceeded five million dollars, and before leaving the insurance field he coined the new generic term "estate planning."

Next Davidson moved into the investment business. He became president of three corporations, chairman of the board of six, and originator of *seven* different bills relating to taxation which he presented before the Senate and

Congressional Committees—and saw them enacted into law.

More than that, Davidson raised $25 million for the original oil funds resulting in 278 successful oil wells! For several years, he wrote a newspaper column, "This Week in Washington with Clinton Davidson," which was carried by 900 newspapers.

What made the difference between the fumbling, inept salesman struggling to boost his earnings to $200 a month —and the astonishingly successful sales and corporate executive?

Clint told me the difference came *when he turned to the Bible for help and committed his life to the Lord.*

Then he explained how surprised he'd been when as a despondent "flop," he discovered in the Bible how Paul had overcome obstacles far greater than his. In fact, Paul had done such a wonderful selling job that his ideas were still "bought" nearly 2,000 years later, by millions upon millions of people!

The astonishing thing to Davidson was the fact that Paul had to sell one of the most *difficult propositions imaginable.* Most of his prospects were heathen who worshiped idols which they could touch and see. He had to persuade them to believe in God, whom they could not see or feel. Not only that, but he faced tremendous opposition. He was slandered, beaten up, jailed. Once he was stoned and dragged out of the city and left for dead.

Yet Paul succeeded remarkably. And the principles Paul employed so effectively became Clint Davidson's. I was fascinated as he outlined the program which led to his incredible success. Davidson came to me two days before the end of 1957.

"You don't know who I am," he said. "But I'd like to offer my services to you. I imagine you've made a lot of money this year."

I admitted that I had.

"Then you will pay a big tax. But if you would like me to

work with you, I believe I can save you some money. It won't cost you a dime."

The next day, this chuckling, round, white-haired gentleman showed me how to save $50,000 on my income tax! That year! So began our relationship, which lasted until his death two years ago. And in the years that followed, he not only became a valued business advisor, but a beloved friend who gradually shared with me some of his rich spiritual insights.

One of the things that impressed me most was Clint's method of praying. When he prayed, it was the most intimate personal conversation with Jesus I had ever heard.

He was a jolly fellow, full of life and love and remarkably vigorous until he died at 73. Very few days went by without the mail bringing a joke or note from him to the girls individually. When he visited in our home, which was often, at the end of the day he would ask happily, "Girls, shall we have a little talk with our Father before you go to bed?"

His personal approach to God wasn't lost on the girls. It was quite a contrast to my prayers, which were all too similar to prayers I had heard over and over in church circles.

Clinton Davidson appeared to get a whole lot more pure joy out of life than I did, although I was much younger! And especially at our times of devotion, I could tell when he sat down he was expecting to enjoy some rich and beautiful experience. He almost glowed. My attitude by contrast was, "Isn't this a good thing we're doing for our kids? I'm sure God is pleased, too."

The curious part about it was that seldom did Davidson put his feelings into words. It wasn't necessary. His presence radiated his love for God and for those he was with.

My manager Jack was suspicious of him for a long time. He couldn't understand how anybody could do so much without being paid for it. And the funny part about it was that Clint didn't say much about his faith, either. He simply lived it. When you were around him, you had the undeniable feeling he was enjoying life far more than you were. But you didn't resent this at all, which is sort of funny in itself.

Humanly speaking, Clint's later life appeared to be centered in a place called Camp Shiloh. This was a retreat center he had established on his own estate on the shore of a beautiful lake in New Jersey.

When Clint and Flora Davidson bought the estate, they decided to share its beauties by developing a camp program for underprivileged ghetto children. The idea was to bring kids out where they could run and play in the outdoors and have the benefits of Bible study and prayer everyday, under spiritual counselors.

All Clint Davidson ever asked from me, in turn for being constantly ready to advise me in business, was that I make a contribution at the end of the year to Camp Shiloh. The amount he always left to me. That's all he asked.

Clint appeared so inwardly serene that I often envied him. On occasion he would tell me how he had been on a rush trip to Chicago or some other city to present an investment program to a group of millionaire clients. The airplane would be delayed, and it looked as though he was going to miss the meeting. At the airport it would be snowing or raining and no cabs in sight. He would breathe a prayer and ask the Lord for help. Unexpectedly a cab would come out of nowhere he would jump in and arrive just in the nick of time. He would thank God, tip the driver and stroll in, chuckling.

Clint Davidson was a giant influence on me, more that I realized then. His quiet radiant confidence in God prepared me in a number of ways for *the revelation which was to change the whole direction of my life.*

I had made a number of different efforts to recapture earlier successes, but they failed. I had also blundered on several important matters, in both my professional career and in business. At this juncture I could have easily gone down the drain spiritually, but Clint Davidson, in his joyful way, came along as plain proof of what great things God can do in the life of a totally committed man, no matter what his business.

I remember times when something good would happen to us, something that seemed like a specific answer to prayer. When we shared this with Clint, he would smile and say, "Yes, I know,". . .as though he was expecting something like this to happen!

I always had the feeling that nothing of a spiritual nature came as a great surprise to him. He seemed to know more than he said. It was through Clint that I first caught glimpses of the fact that God could work miracles—even in our day! On several occasions he had alluded to the fact that God had touched the body of his wife, Flora. I only knew that she walked with a cane, although she never complained in any way.

Then one time when we were together in our den, the subject of physical healing came up. In his quiet way he told me how he had offered to help the evangelist, Oral Roberts, with his financial structure, just as he'd helped me. As a result, he had been impressed with Roberts' ministry of praying for the sick. Later, back home in New Jersey, while watching Roberts on his TV program, Clint got the impression, which he believed came from the Lord, that he and Flora should attend one of the evangelistic meetings, where Oral would be speaking and praying for the sick. However, the meetings were then going on in Kansas City!

Flora had been in an accident some years before and her hip had been seriously injured. The pain had increased until it became agonizing. Despite everything the physicians attempted, x-rays disclosed that the composition of the bone was deteriorating. Finally their decision was that the only thing to be done was to fuse the hip into a rigid position. They admitted this might not ease the pain; it would only enable her to remain somewhat mobile.

Flora Davidson has told me since then that as they talked and prayed about attending the meeting, she became convinced that God was going to heal her. So they took the long train ride and attended the meeting on two different nights. When she was prayed for the first evening, she felt no relief. The next evening she said she felt a slight tremor in her hip, but that was all. She was not aware of what happened until she awakened the next morning to realize that *she had slept through the first night in over a year without pain!*

In the days that immediately followed she gained strength rapidly. Now the pain was *completely gone* and she was able to move about easily with only the aid of a cane!

When they returned to the physician he was astonished, and insisted on making another x-ray. When he compared the two, it was obvious that the deterioration had not only stopped, *but the tissues were in the process of rebuilding.*

"I don't understand it," he said. "It must be a miracle."

As I listened to Clint in our den, I'll admit it was hard to believe. Here was a millionaire business man, a business consultant to men whose combined worth was over 300 million, a Washington consultant and financial brain telling me he had *seen* miracles of healing.

But this was only the beginning for me.

A few months later I was on my way to Mexico City for a 10-day appearance. At a newsstand in the airport, I picked up a paperback book entitled *The Cross and the Switchblade.* Here again I was astonished to find accounts of how a minister had prayed for young people trapped by narcotic addictions, *and how God had healed and delivered them.* The whole book read like a modern day sequel to the Acts of the Apostles in the New Testament!

I was intrigued by these miracles that were coming in direct answer to the prayers of David Wilkerson, the young minister who wrote the book.

Later when Clint Davidson and I were together I asked him if he had ever read the book. He had. And, as a matter of fact, he contacted Wilkerson for me when I explained I thought the story ought to be filmed. Although we were able to get an option on the book for movie rights, I was unable at the time to find anyone in Hollywood interested in making the movie. The uniform response was that "religion is poison at the box-office."

These events, and my contacts with people who not only believed the Bible, but who actually had seen Bible-type miracles take place today, stirred a hunger in my own mind and heart to have a similar relationship with God. Often I had said to myself, "If I could just see *one miracle,* have *one experience* like the people in the Bible—I'd have the same faith they had!"

To Shirley, Clint Davidson was a living example of the Christian life she was looking for. Little did either of us know then that we were about to experience the reality of the presence of the Lord in *our* lives—in the same way that Clint and Flora had!

CHAPTER 10

CAN THIS BE TRUE?

I hadn't really prayed much for a long time. Even when I thought about it, I'd shrug the idea away. What right did I have to ask God for anything? Sometimes I'd stand outside at night, looking up at the stars, almost feeling the earth turn — and wonder if He still knew my name. I wanted to offer God something, somehow — but what did I have left that mattered to Him?

So when the taping of my first NBC daytime TV show was set for Sunday, I insisted that the schedule be arranged so I could attend church in Burbank. This was no big deal, I knew that — but I wanted God to know that I was willing to be counted on His side again. On the way back from church to the final rehearsal and taping, I prayed out loud as I drove along in·the car. *It was the first time I had ever simply talked to God,* in such a conversational way.

"Father, I've really drifted away, haven't I? Is there a way back? I've made an awful lot of mistakes, I know — but I do want to serve you again. I'm sorry for all the things I've done and said, sorry that I've practically frittered away the inheritance you've given me. I pray that you'll bless this show today. . .and if you do. . .that you'll use it and me in your will, and most of all. . .that you'll draw me closer to you. I need you, Father. . .I need you. . . ."

As I prayed, "I need you, Father. . .I need you. . ." the strangest thing — tears rolled down my cheeks.

It was quite an experience. Just driving along and talking aloud to God in the car, and *hearing myself pray.*

Before this, even in a hotel room alone when I prayed, it would be in whispers, and rather stilted at that. I had no real idea, yet, of how very close a person can come to his Lord. So far as I knew, the long-distance partnership that I'd experienced earlier in life was about as close as you could get. Now I was sort of placing a station-to-station call again, and praying with the sort of naive faith that Shirley and I had together in the early days of our marriage. The only difference was that now I was driving along in a Cadillac in Burbank, instead of being on my knees in the rickety apartment in Texas.

I'll have to admit it was partly a selfish prayer. I was asking for help, because I'd tasted *enough* flops and failures, based on my reason and the abilities of my agents and producers. Now I was starting to re-focus on the fact that if God were there and still listening to me, that He was able to do things that ability, intellect, experience could not do! I had been spiritually blind—now I was beginning to see. Those tears were spiritual eye-drops, I guess.

The NBC show was sold and went on the air immediately, where it remained for a full season! Even after the cancellation notice went out, the ratings continued to go up. I believe the network people regretted their decision to cancel during the last 13-week period. But I completed the show, and that led to an hour and a half syndicated show which began almost immediately.

Meanwhile, several years before I had met another man who was to exert a great influence on my spiritual life as well as Clint Davidson. This was George Otis, a business man, former president of Lear and now a business developer and broker.

I had bought an Apollo sports car, a racy job built in Italy and powered with a Buick engine. Otis had become interested in the Apollo, and was considering buying into the company. He learned I had bought an Apollo and called to find out how I liked it. As a result of the conversation my agent agreed that this might be a good investment for me also. We checked Otis' business record, and agreed that if he were to take over and run the operation, it might be a big money-maker. Accordingly, Otis went to Italy and visited the factory. On his return, he came over to the house to discuss the matter, and Shirley sat in on the meeting.

During that visit, Otis related to us the story of his own conversion to Jesus Christ. (As we discovered, with George there's no separation between business and God.) In the course of the conversation I asked him whether he had read *The Cross and the Switchblade,* the book I had picked up on the newsstand on my way to Mexico City several months before.

When he said he had, I told him how excited I was about the book's movie possibilities. This was during the period when Clint Davidson was working on the option to the film rights.

But Otis pointed out that it would be very difficult for me to play such a part until I came to know the Holy Spirit in the same way in which David Wilkerson, the author of the book, knew Him. Even from a "method acting" viewpoint, this made sense.

In the first place, God had answered Wilkerson's prayers in many specific and supernatural ways, and obviously I didn't believe the Bible that way. In other words, we differed in our understanding of what the Bible teaches regarding "miracles." He believed that could happen today; I wasn't so sure. Yet, I had to admit that God had honored and *answered his prayers* in more miraculous ways than I had ever experienced or thought possible!

Secondly, the curious report that boys in the streets of Harlem and Brooklyn were "baptized with the Holy Spirit" and then spoke in other languages or "tongues" was beyond me. Was Wilkerson lying about this, or imagining things? This seemed so far out that no "sensible" person could possibly understand it. At the same time, the descriptions of those experiences in the ghetto streets touched me deeply.

You see, I've always been taught that we take the Holy Spirit in us as we read the Word of God, the Bible. The Spirit is in the Word, and as we make the Word of God a part of our daily lives, to that degree the Spirit dwells in us. The Spirit is contained in the Word, and if the Word guides us, then we can truly say that the Spirit is guiding us.

Also the doctrinal authorities in the Church of Christ believe that all things supernatural *vanished by the end of the first century.* After the last apostle died, the power to pass on miracle-working ability to someone else ceased. The working of miracles, which the apostles and the disciples of the first century performed, was limited to the record of them in the Scriptures. That is, when the Apostle John finished writing the last words of the Book of the Revelation on the Isle of Patmos, there was no need for the Word of God to be confirmed further with signs and wonders. The record is now completed.

This has been our Church of Christ thinking and our position.

Besides, the whole idea of "miracles," "tongues" and charismatic gifts left a bad taste in our mouths, because we had the image of people rolling on the ground, kicking their feet and shouting "hallelujah."

No, all we needed existed right there in the Word of God. If we soberly and devotedly lived by that Word, that was all there was to it. So-called "miracles" and "speaking in tongues" had to be from the devil—or people's own minds.

The disturbing thing about Wilkerson's book was that he was continually risking *his life* on the proposition that *God does perform miracles today.* As a result, his story is crammed with answered prayer, changed lives, healings, Divine interventions—and he gives names, dates and places!

So first came Clint Davidson, then David Wilkerson; both saying that *God is alive today,* and that He's ready to respond to our prayers, that we can see in our day *the same mighty power* at work as the men and women of the first century saw. And now here's George Otis, another successful business man, sitting in the same chair in my den where Clint has stunned me a couple of years before. He's telling me about the *same power* of God in *his life!* Now, George Otis is no kook or odd ball—he's a man who serves as a business "doctor." He takes over ailing companies, removes the diseased parts, and brings in new management. When the company gets on its feet, he goes on to something else. A highly respected, analytical kind of guy, a man who can't afford to be fooled. And in broad daylight and in a business suit—not in a late night ghost-storytelling session —Otis is saying that *God performs miracles today!*

He related how once he had no place for God in his life. Then, how he became a nominal or middleground Christian, like I was right then. Finally, how when he made a *total surrender* as the result of a series of calamities and frustrations, *his whole life was changed.* His relationships with God, his family and friends became supercharged with power; his business career flourished. Now God was his partner, "a Partner who knows tomorrow!"

Otis' account stirred me, I couldn't get it out of my mind. I began to wonder if I'd ever be able to see miracles happen in my life. I knew that I needed a few.

After the Apollo episode, and while I was still out at the NBC studios, I bought a Ferrari in Italy and had it equipped with a full stereo rig. George Otis had started a little company devoted to putting the Bible on records and on tape, called Bible Voice. He gave me a whole box of tape cartridges on which the New Testament in modern language had been recorded. I really didn't think I'd listen to them often, but I put a couple of the cartridges in the glove compartment of the Ferrari. Occasionally, while driving out to Burbank, I woud listen to one and really enjoy it!

One day when I was filming the *Perils of Pauline* on the Universal lot, a couple of friends came along to watch. After lunch in the commissary we got into the Ferrari and headed out to the set.

"Listen to this," I said as I flipped on the stereo.

My friends began to laugh. "Who'd ever believe this? We're on the lot at Universal, riding in a Ferrari and listening to the Bible — in stereo!"

Of course, my interest in listening to the Bible was only occasional so far, but whenever I flipped on that Bible recording, a sort of peace drifted into the car — despite crowded traffic and the speed at which I usually travel. When I was under pressure, especially, I knew I could slip that tape in, and as I listened, began not to worry so much about whether I arrived home on time or what would happen after I got there. My Ferrari became a virtual sanctuary.

CHAPTER 11

THE DARKEST HOUR

Home, now, had become anything *but* a sanctuary. I was sporadically struggling to get back to shore while Shirley remained adrift and "confused." She really seemed to function much better when I was gone — and she let me know it. With me out of town, she didn't have to make decisions about parties and prayers, drinking and doctrine, "beautiful people" and church people. She simply concentrated on holding the family together, solving the girls problems, going through the motions of daily life. Her relationship with God would have to wait. There seemed no way to have God, family, career and me in one package.

One of the ragged nerve-ends in her agony was remembering that most of her rules of Christian living had originally come from *me*, and my background! The Foley home had been permissive. Her parents saw nothing wrong in either drinking or smoking, but Shirley had never become hooked, mainly because she wasn't interested — not because she saw anything wrong in them. And dancing just naturally was a vital and enjoyable thing to her. But since I objected to all of these things and had convincing arguments about each one, she willingly gave them up so that we could have a harmonious home and family life.

Now when she asked that I give up drinking, smoking, gambling in Las Vegas and other things—for the same basic reason—she couldn't understand why I wasn't willing to do it. Hadn't she already given up a way of life that would have been easy and natural, because of her love for me? Now she was asking me to give up a way of life which she saw threatening our home, our love, our very existence together—a way of life strikingly similar to the one she'd given up when we married—and I just couldn't see it!

I thought she was wrong to put it on this basis. It was *my* money. I could *afford* to lose a few dollars. I wasn't *hurting* anybody and to ask me to give up something that I enjoyed, because she thought it was wrong, was putting an unnecessary strain on our relationship. Shirley actually began to wonder if I really loved her.

And finally, the very thing she thought could *never* happen was happening. Her love, for me and for her children, was slipping from her. A "grayness" was setting in. The things she'd done freely and willingly for years, because of her love for us, she now found difficult to do. They became a burden, a chore. What was all the effort *for,* anyway?

At the same time she continued to plead with God for the return of this love—both on my part and hers—not realizing that she had let these physical relationships get ahead of her relationship to the Lord Himself. She even came to the point (which I had passed sometime before) where she began to deny her relationship to the Lord.

The blackest, most soul-rending moment arrived when at a party a Hollywood personality asked, "I hear you and

Pat are quite religious. Is that so?"

Her answer simply was, "Well. . .*Pat's* religious."

She has told me since then that she could hear herself talking, but just couldn't believe that the words were hers. Hours later she was in tears as she realized that she, like Peter, had actually denied her faith in Jesus.

Then a curious thing began to happen. As I began to share with her the conversations I was having with George Otis, and of the Bible tapes I was listening to in the car, she reacted negatively! Now that she found herself cut off, drifting, purposeless — "lost in the stars," where I'd left her — she resented my growing hunger for direction, my attempts to find God. We were still so out of step; our roles had reversed, and I was leaving her behind again. It was a bitter irony.

Finally, one day she got down on her face before the Lord and, sobbing, confessed to Him that she did not love me as she once did. . .but that with His help she would never let me or anyone else know it. She knew that God meant marriage to be a life-time covenant, so love me or not, she'd make-believe and do her best the rest of her life — not because she wanted to, but because she believed this was what God demanded.

And to help her do this, she started reading books on spiritual themes. She took a greater interest in church activities, and spent more time with Christian people. I was encouraged, not realizing the bleakness of her spirit.

Along about this time, I made a tough move — a public confession of sin in front of the whole church! The NBC show I had prayed about had been produced. God had done His part; now I knew I had to do mine.

I thought, "Shirley knows about most of my mistakes, if not all of 'em. She knows I've been a 'weak sister' spiritually. My kids know I haven't been the best father to them. And a few of the folks in the church know of the compromises I've made. I've sort of let everybody down, really. I've got to begin somewhere, and confessing publicly to your brethren in the church is what the Bible says to do (James 5:16). At least, maybe they'll pray for me."

On the way to church next Sunday, I told Shirley and the girls what I was going to do. No one said much the rest of the way there.

I confessed my failures publicly that morning, choking back my own tears, and expressed my gratitude to Shirley for standing by me. But afterward, she was strangely cool; in fact, she resented the whole deal. I think her resentment was more in personal remorse than anything else, though. As she said later, a whole bitter flood of her own misdeeds passed before her eyes. She felt condemned even more by my public praise, and her heart tore as she thought of the poor influence she'd been on many others. Yet there was nothing she could do about them now.

Except—pray for them, which she began to do, earnestly and deeply, and does to this day. Obviously, God heard these prayers and responded, bringing most of these people back into her life—but only after He drew her back to Himself.

Shirley's longing was climaxed one night when she went to church alone while I was taping a show. Normally, we sat in the first or second row from the front; this night she slipped in at the back, because she felt so miserable.

The message was on *total commitment* to Jesus Christ. The struggle began in her mind and heart as the message went on. That deep, universal hunger for "oneness" with God was welling up like a fountain; she felt that she must make a confession and total surrender to the Lord. Yet the question loomed into her mind, as it always does when we face such decisions: "What will people think if Mrs. Pat Boone makes a confession? Will they assume worse things than I've actually done?" Even church folks often judge women more harshly than men.

Then the Lord whispered to her spirit, "Are you doing it

94

for them or are you doing it for Me?"

In desperation when the invitation came, she struggled to her feet. After walking what seemed like 40 miles, to the front row, she felt an irresistable desire to kneel. *Yet we don't kneel in the Church of Christ;* it seems "denominational," "overly-emotional." What would they think? Again the whisper "Are you doing it for them or are you doing it for Me?"

Shirley knelt in front of the entire congregation.

As she's often said since then, the whole world didn't suddenly become beautiful. But now, for the first time in many months, Shirley discovered that God was as near as her own heartbeat when she needed help. She stumbled many times, but whenever she did, she found Him ready to lift her up and encourage her along the way.

Also for the first time in many months, she began to read the Bible for a better understanding of the Lord. She was confident that she knew God, the Father. She was also certain that she knew God the Son, Jesus Christ, because she had accepted Him as her Savior and her Lord. But she did not know God the Holy Spirit. Lately she'd heard me talk about Him, and she had met a few people who talked about His presence as a reality, as a guide and counselor in the everyday problems of life.

As she read the Word of God, she began to see that the Holy Spirit was as personal as God and Jesus Christ. Jesus talked about Him as the *revealer of truth.* So she prayed that she might understand all that this truth should mean to her. She also began to borrow the Bible tapes, and use them in the stereo in *her* car, as I was now doing.

What she came to learn is the beautiful fact that *when you know the Holy Spirit,* He gives you a love for people that you can't understand or explain yourself! And of course, this was what was about to happen in our family relationship. As the Bible plainly says in Romans 5:5, ". . .because the love of God has been poured out within our hearts

95

through the Holy Spirit who was given to us."

Like all of us, Shirley had to learn that she must first love God *above everything else.* That's the Universal Key—the unconditional opening of the door. When that happened, then He could open her eyes and heart and mind to the fullness of the Holy Spirit, so that His love would then be "poured out" in her heart for those about her.

Now we were bumping into more and more people who had an awareness of the Holy Spirit as a living reality! As I listened to the Bible tapes, I was impressed at how many times the Holy Spirit is mentioned in the New Testament. He's on almost every page!! Also I saw that Jesus always referred to the Holy Spirit as He—not "it"—*He!* The Holy Spirit is the third *person* of the Godhead!

Shirley too was coming to this awareness. Up to this time she'd never been much of a reader. Now she was hungrily reading the Bible, pouring over it, devouring it —and *understanding* it!

What we both wanted now was more of a sense of direction, more faith. Both of us were groping and searching. I knew Paul had said in Romans 10:17 that "faith comes by hearing the Word of God." We were doing that literally! Then one day Shirley came to me with a statement she'd found: "Hope is the antechamber to faith."

This was a ray of light. You start out by hoping, and you feed that hope a batch of God's word, especially His promises to a believer. Then while you're waiting for something to happen, as you continue to hope, God has opportunity to turn that hope into *faith!* Later, I discovered that the author of the book of Hebrews had said it even better. "Now faith is the assurance of things hoped for, the conviction of things not seen" (Hebrews 11:1).

And imagine this, Shirley began to show me things *I* had never noticed in the Bible! This was funny. Here I was supposed to be the resident Bible scholar, but it was Shirley, the nonreader, who was coming up with things from the Word of God that I had completely overlooked.

On my own now, I was reading the book, *They Speak With Other Tongues*, by John Sherrill. I was astonished at the way in which an experienced author, journalist, and editor of *Guideposts* magazine, had documented the case for the biblical experience "speaking in tongues" for our day. This distinguished Episcopalian writer had begun his study for a magazine article on this controversial "phenomenon;" he was certain that it was a peculiar psychological game. But by the time he had completed his research, to his astonishment he discovered that today, in virtually every major Christian group. . .Catholic, Episcopal. Presbyterian, Methodist, Baptist, Lutheran, Congregational—an increasing number of men and women were discovering the reality of the Holy Spirit, were seeing miracles performed as the result of prayer, and were relating to their heavenly Father through a prayer language. His discoveries eventually led Sherrill to *experience these things himself* in a new relationship to God!

I went back through David Wilkerson's book, *The Cross and the Switchblade* and now I was getting goosebumps on top of goosebumps!

These books, together with my conversations with George Otis, were leading me to do a great deal of thinking about my relationship to the Holy Spirit. An expectancy was growing. . .was it hope?

I remembered an incredible conversation I'd had a number of years ago with Harris Goodwin, the young associate minister of the Hollywood Church of Christ. Harris Goodwin had begun to have trouble with his voice, and was constantly hoarse. When the doctor examined him, the smear test showed him that he had cancer of the esophagus. The physician told him his only hope was to have the larynx removed. When Goodwin explained he was a preacher, and *could not do without a voice*, the physician only shook his head, and said "I'm sorry."

So Goodwin went home and prayed, "Lord, if you want to take me, I'm ready to go. But I am not going to let anyone take my voice from me. If I live, I'm going to preach the Gospel, and *I can't do that without a voice.* I leave it up to you."

Since he was having so much trouble preaching, he went to work in a jewelry store in Beverly Hills. Gradually, he noticed the hoarseness was disappearing. He returned to the doctor for an examination.

"I don't understand it. There simply is no trace of that cancer!" said the doctor.

Today Harris Goodwin is preaching in Mexico City. We hear from him occasionally, and when I visited Mexico I spent a little time with him. He doesn't talk about it, and neither had I; who'd believe it? And yet, it happened.

Well, now I was really in earnest, and praying that the Lord would help me make my life count for something again; that He'd really take over and guide me. Occasionally I prayed that if the relationship with the Holy Spirit was real —that He'd help me to understand it.

One evening when Shirley was away, I actually got down on my face in the den to "humble myself." I also prayed that God would give me this "prayer language" but nothing happened.

I realize now that I was asking for a *gift,* and not actually surrendering myself to the Giver of all good gifts. I wanted a confirmation *before* I'd made a commitment.

But I was learning a whole lot more about prayer! In New York I met with David Wilkerson and some of his financial advisors to discuss the possibility of filming *The Cross and the Switchblade.* Here, for the first time, I heard responsive prayer. That is, while one man prayed, the others responded and joined in: "Yes, Lord." Or "Thank you, Jesus," etc. Many of these grown men were weeping! I was so impressed with the warmth of this sort of prayer, that when I returned

98

home, I suggested we try to make our family prayer time more meaningful and spontaneous in this way. Right away, our prayer life took on new dimension.

By this time, Shirley was asking God to take over completely in her life. Suddenly, when she opened herself to the Holy Spirit, He spoke to her in an astonishingly different and wonderful way.

CHAPTER 12

SHIRLEY BEGINS TO SEE

It was a sunny morning early in the summer of 1968, while I was away on some appearances. Shirley was serving breakfast in our home in Beverly Hills to George Otis and his wife, Virginia, and a long time friend Merlyn Lund. It had been Shirley's idea, her way of introducing these special God-loving people to each other. Each of them has a special "glow," a warmth, an ability to love and see beyond the superficial in others, a confidence—and a contagious sort of happiness! She thought they should know one another, so she arranged it, secretly hoping (I think) to discover what gave them their joyful radiance.

After breakfast the four of them sat around the table with open Bibles.

As Shirley described it to me, they talked about what it really meant to be a Christian. They agreed that this involved acknowledging that Jesus Christ is the Son of God, —and that God sent Him to live as a man among other men so that He could identify with our human natures. (Hebrews 2:14-18).

Every honest man admits that he commits sin. According to the Bible, sin, which originated with Satan, separates us from the perfect God and the blessings of His love. Only God, *because* He loves us, could, or *would,* have devised the "rescue plan" through which we can be brought back into fellowship with Him.

To save us, He allowed Jesus Christ to suffer at the very hands of Satan, so that in His fleshly nature He was tempted by the Devil himself, tortured by the men of His day, and eventually was put to death. In submitting to this death, Jesus paid the price for the sin of all mankind. "But we do see Him who has been made for a little while lower than the angels, namely, Jesus, because of the suffering of death crowned with glory and honor, that by the grace of God He might taste death for every one" (Hebrews 2:9).

Satan thought he'd won! With Jesus on the cross, he thought he'd defeated God! *But,* because Jesus Christ was the Son of God, He was given the power to rise from the dead—to walk triumphantly out of Hell by His own power. When Christ conquered Satan, He made it possible for all men thereafter, who believed in Him as Messiah, also to receive the power of God to live a joyous life of victory over sin in this world, and to have the certainty of eternal life with God thereafter.

They agreed that this was the basic gospel or "good news" which all Protestant denominations, as well as the Roman Catholic church recognize. It was George who pointed out that the basis for this "rescue plan" of Jesus Christ is explained in I Corinthians 15:3-4. Here Paul says, "For I delivered you as of first importance what I also received, that Christ died for our sins according to the Scriptures, and that He was buried, and that He was raised on the third day according to the Scriptures."

So undeniably, our faith is based on the *Divine person of Jesus Christ:* who He is, what He did and what He expects *us* to do. Now neither Shirley nor I doubted that we'd been

102

Christians for a long time. Intellectually, by sheer faith, we'd claimed Him as Savior and physically we'd been baptized. In some churches this is referred to as being "saved" or "born again." Other churches call it becoming a "believer" or "being converted."

Whatever the terminology, the point is that we each must at some point in our lives, acknowledge that Jesus Christ, the Son of God, lived as a human being on earth, died and rose again. And we have to put our personal confidence in Him as Savior. The Bible makes this plain, "That if you confess with your mouth Jesus as Lord, and believe in your heart that God raised Him from the dead, *you shall be saved"* (Romans 10:9). All this we'd done.

Their discussion that morning, however, centered around the person of the Holy Spirit. Who, or what was He? What did, or does, He do? We'd always had just a vague concept of some unseen "force" that had inspired Scripture and caused miraculous things in the first century.

As we'd been reading the Bible and seeking truth in recent months, however, we'd seen Jesus and all His disciples refer to God's Holy Spirit as "Him" and "He"—a Divine personality. In fact, in John 16:7, Jesus told His disciples that it was necessary that He leave the earth or "the Helper shall not come to you; but if I go, I will send Him to you." Unto whom—just to the apostles? Obviously, no.

Now the Otises and Merlyn from their own experience were telling Shirley about a deeper and more beautiful relationship with God—through this very Holy Spirit!

"But didn't I receive the Holy Spirit when I believed in Jesus and was baptized?" Shirley asked.

They turned in their Bibles to Acts 2:38, 39 which reads: "And Peter said to them, 'Repent and let each of you be baptized in the name of Jesus Christ for the forgiveness of your sins; and you shall receive the gift of the Holy Spirit. For the promise is for you and your children, and for all who are far off, as many as the Lord our God shall call to

Himself." Obviously then, Shirley could see that when she had received Jesus Christ and had been baptized in His name, then the Holy Spirit was hers—by right and promise!

Jesus had promised this on the night of His betrayal when He was talking to His disciples. "And I will ask the Father, and He will give you another Helper, that He may be with you forever; that is the Spirit of truth, whom the world cannot receive, because it does not behold Him or know Him, but you know Him because He abides with you, and will be *in* you" (John 14:16-17).

Then George explained how some Christians of that day who had believed in Jesus and acknowledged Him as the Christ, their Savior, nevertheless remained ignorant about the Holy Spirit. Somebody had to teach them. He read from the 8th chapter of Acts, verses 14 through 19.

"Now when the apostles in Jerusalem heard that Samaria had received the word of God, they sent them Peter and John, who came down and prayed for them, that they might receive the Holy Spirit. For He had not yet fallen upon any of them; and they had simply been baptized in the name of the Lord Jesus. Then they began laying their hands on them, and they were receiving the Holy Spirit. Now when Simon saw that the Spirit was bestowed through the laying on of the apostles' hands, he offered them money, saying, "Give this authority to me as well, so that everyone on whom I lay my hands may receive the Holy Spirit."

In other words, the people at Samaria had been converted, and baptized in the water by Philip the evangelist, and yet had not received the completeness of the Holy Spirit until Peter and John taught them, prayed for them, and in this case, laid their hands upon them.

In their Bibles again, they saw how a similar situation developed in the 19th chapter of Acts. This time Paul found a group of disciples in the city of Ephesus. He asked them, "Did you receive the Holy Spirit when you believed?" (This implies that Paul realized they *might* have.) They explained

104

that they had been baptized only in John the Baptist's baptism—for repentance from sin.

Shirley knew that John the Baptist, who had preceded Jesus, said that he baptized with water, but that one greater than he would come who would baptize *with the Holy Ghost and with fire!* (Matthew 3:11).

The Bible records that when these believers in the city of Ephesus heard this, "They were baptized in the name of the Lord Jesus. And when Paul had laid his hands upon them, the Holy Spirit came on them, and they began speaking with tongues and prophesying" (Acts 19:5-6).

For the first time Shirley began to see that *there must be a difference* between water baptism and being baptized with the Holy Ghost.

Shirley had been baptized in water years ago. Was there more?

"What's the difference between being a baptized believer, and being baptized with the Holy Ghost?" she asked.

As they looked through the Bible, they found several indications of what the answer might be.

When Jesus promised His disciples (John 14:16,17,20) that He'd give them the Comforter, or Holy Spirit, He said, "But you know him because He abides with you, and *will* be *in* you. "In that day you shall know that I am in My Father, and you in Me, and I in you."

Then over in the letter written to the churches in Galatia, they noted the question, "Did you receive the Spirit by the works of the law, or by hearing with faith?" (Galatians 3:2).

From all these scriptures, it seemed obvious that the baptized believer *does* receive the Holy Spirit in some measure—at least in the *right to ask* for the in-dwelling, the fullness of Christ in us which is described as the baptism of the Holy Spirit in the Bible. Could it be that water baptism is something *we* do in repentance and obedience—and that the baptism of the Spirit is something only Christ Him-

self can do? (Matthew 3:11). And that *faith in Jesus'
promise* causes us to ask for, receive and exercise this gift?

As these things unfolded before Shirley, her excitement
grew, because she knew that Jesus had promised His
disciples, "But ye shall receive *power,* when the Holy Spirit
has come upon you" (Acts 1:8).

Power—to live a consistent Christian life. Power
—to share the reality of a risen Lord more effectively with
others. For Jesus continues His statement, "And ye shall be
witnesses unto me both in Jerusalem, and in all Judea, and
in Samaria, and unto the uttermost part of the earth."

And George thrilled her by pointing out that when Peter
(Acts 2:39) promised the Holy Ghost to believers, he added
"for the promise is unto you, and to your children, and unto
all that are afar off, even *as many as the Lord our God shall
call!"* Power!

Shirley knew this is what she needed. Her faith was weak,
her family life unravelling. Her love for me and her children
was draining away—and none of her friends, she felt, could
possibly see the evidence of a risen Lord in her life.

The hope was rising in her that *this morning,* by faith
(Galatians 3:2), she might receive the person of the Holy
Spirit *in* her and thus begin to experience a new, greater
and more wonderful relationship with God.

But how would she know it? Was it something you could
feel?

Merlyn and George pointed out that since Jesus is the
Baptizer, He would decide what she would experience; but
they read some Scriptures about the *most common* mani-
festation of the baptism—the praise in another language,
or speaking in tongues.

In Mark 16:17 they read that Jesus said as part of the
Great Commission, *"In My name they will cast out demons,
they will speak with new tongues."* Also in I Corinthians
14:5 they read that the apostle Paul said, "Now I wish that
you all spoke in tongues," and in I Corinthians 14:18, "I thank

106

God, *I speak in tongues more than you all."*

Isn't this what had happened to the Christians in Samaria and Ephesus, which she'd just read about? Now they turned to Acts 10 and read the story of the Roman centurion, Cornelius. Specifically, the 44th through the 46th verses pointed out that, "while Peter was still speaking these words, the Holy Spirit fell upon all those who were listening to the message...for they were hearing them speaking with tongues and *exalting God."*

These Scriptures, which Shirley had known for years, were taking on new depth, new immediacy and excitement. In the Church of Christ, as in most Protestant and Catholic churches, praying or speaking in an unknown language is considered just a 1st century phenomenon. In fact, in most of organized Christianity, it is often ridiculed or criticized as being improper.

Yet as she read her Bible that morning, Shirley was astonished at the many references to "speaking in tongues" and the baptism in the Spirit. There was so much Scripture about something that *"ended in the 1st century!"* Peculiar, wasn't it?

I'd taught her myself the "church position" on the gifts of the Spirit, listed in I Corinthians 12. We believed that when the beloved apostle John, exiled on the Isle of Patmos, wrote the last words of the Revelation—and God's Word was completed—that miraculous or supernatural gifts from the Holy Spirit ceased; they weren't needed any more.

This is what we'd believed; but when Shirley mentioned it, George said, "Not needed anymore? Shirley, the Bible— God's Word—is under attack today from every quarter. Atheists, communists, humanists, many college and high school teachers—and even "liberal" *churchmen*—are denying the inspiration of the Bible. Whole generations of young people are growing up thinking that this book is just a quaint old collection of poems, myths and legends. Even their parents aren't sure that it's relevant to today. The Divine Word *needs confirming*—right now—just as much as it did 2000 years ago!"

"Besides," he continued, "Jesus, in Mark 16, said that signs and wonders would follow 'them that believe'—in practically the same breath as 'he that believeth and is baptized shall be saved!' If belief and baptism are for today, as we all understand—then so are 'signs' that *follow* belief, including 'speaking with new tongues.' Jesus didn't put a 1900-year barrier between verse 16 and verse 17; but men have!"

And then this dynamic Christian added, "Besides, Jesus said exactly what He meant: 'these signs,' wrought by God's Spirit, 'will accompany those who have *believed!*' Believe not only in Christ, but in His promise to 'be in you,' to give you 'power,' to confirm His word 'with signs following.' Few Christians really believe today. They certainly don't have faith enough to 'receive the Spirit' in His supernatural fullness—and Jesus promised those 'signs' only to 'them that *believe!*'"

Suddenly, it was so plain, so simple.

Then they read the first verse of the 14th chapter of I Corinthians. "Pursue love, yet desire earnestly spiritual gifts, but especially that you may prophesy." The Apostle Paul seemed to be issuing a directive—but was he to her?

I studied Greek three years in college and though I'm no scholar, when I later on looked up this verse I discovered that the mood of the verb "desire" is the same as our English *imperative.* In other words, Paul is urging, almost commanding Christians to *desire* spiritual gifts, gifts which the Holy Spirit alone can provide. Wouldn't this include speaking in tongues, as well as prophecy and the other gifts listed in the 12th chapter of I Corinthians? What other answer *could* there be?

The very air in the breakfast room seemed charged with excitement; Shirley felt expectancy welling up within her. She sensed that she was about to meet Jesus as her baptizer in the Holy Spirit.

108

CHAPTER 13

DAY OF REJOICING

Within two hours, by long-distance phone, Shirley was telling me about her experience. "I couldn't wait until George and Merlyn were gone, so that I could be alone with the Lord! Pat, you know that for months I've been crying out to Him for help. At first I thought that what I wanted most in the world was to preserve my family, and our relationship as husband and wife.

"I still wanted these things, but I finally realized that more than anything else, I simply needed the Lord. I needed Jesus!

"If that involved speaking in tongues in order to better worship Him, if Jesus would give me that ability, wonderful! I wanted the others to leave so I could go up to my room and pray."

As a matter of fact, this is what George had told Shirley to do.

"You don't need anybody to help you," he said. "This is between you and Jesus. Simply give yourself to the Lord in complete surrender of mind, will, heart, and voice. He'll put words of praise and thanksgiving into your heart and they'll come out in a beautiful language that you may not be able to understand, at least with your mind. The Holy Spirit will help you to express feelings too deep in meaning to be comprehended by mere man."

I've come to realize since then that some people make the mistake of seeking gifts of the Holy Spirit simply for the sake of having them. Usually they are disappointed.

God doesn't give us spiritual gifts just for our own enjoyment. Instead He gives us special abilities so that we can better worship and serve Him. That's where the real enjoyment is! This is what Jesus meant when He told the early disciples that they would be baptized with the Holy Ghost so that they might receive power; power to serve, power to overcome — power to become! This is why some Bible scholars have said, "Don't seek gifts, but the Giver."

They're absolutely right! When our heart's desire is to have a closer relationship with Jesus Christ, above all other things, then we are in the best possible position to receive the baptism in the Holy Spirit and the gifts He may provide.

And this is what happened to Shirley that morning in her room. When she opened her heart to God in an earnest desire to praise Him, He answered.

Jesus said, in His sermon on the Mount, "Blessed are those who hunger and thirst for righteousness, for they shall be satisfied" (Matthew 5:6).

"All I wanted was more of Jesus," Shirley says. "Whatever it took, I was willing. I prayed He would forgive me of every sin I had committed, and named everything I could think of — from the worst to the least, even to reading the horoscope. I wanted to be forgiven of anything that possibly could stand in my way of coming to Him in this new and beautiful dimension."

Even though she didn't understand exactly what was happening, she prayed, "Jesus, I need you — and only You.

You said that if I ask for bread You wouldn't give me a stone. And if I ask for fish You wouldn't give me a serpent. I don't want anything from Satan, I don't want some psychological counterfeit. I'm offering You my voice, my lips, my soul, my life. I want to give all of me to You. I know Your Spirit has been *with* me, and in me but please, dear Lord, now I need Your Spirit to fill me.

"If you have another language for me, I want it—but only if it's from You. I want You to *baptize me in Your Holy Spirit*—as You promised."

And then when she'd said all she knew to say, she offered her voice, making soft sounds, mostly vowels, knowing it was all her own effort, but also knowing it was a step of faith, reaching out for Jesus. And He met her! It was suddenly no longer her effort at all. It seemed that "rivers of living water" were flowing from her, washing her clean. She heard herself speaking faster than she thought humanly possible, and as the Lord gave her freedom of expression, His Holy Spirit began to bear witness with her spirit. She was overcome by the sense of the presence of the Lord and an overwhelming feeling of love.

"The amazing thing that happened to me was that I felt myself *immersed in love.* I don't know how else to explain it. We talk about being baptized or totally immersed in water. I was totally immersed in love. It was so beautiful," she says.

In the peaceful stillness that followed, Shirley looked at her watch. She'd been praying forty-five minutes, yet it seemed like only five.

Then she called me on the telephone in San Antonio where I was on tour. As soon as I heard her voice, I could tell she was deeply moved, that something had happened.

She said, "Darling, are you alone?"

I told her I was.

"It's happened. It's real."

"What's real?" I asked.

Then she told me how the Lord had met her and showed her His love for her in a new way. She told me also how much more she loved me and the children, that everything seemed so different.

I had the old goose-bumps again!

"Well, honey, that's great," I said. "I don't doubt it at all; I'm thrilled for you, and, Shirley, my time is coming—because I want to know this love for Him and you, too."

While I was still in San Antonio, I prayed for the gift of the Holy Spirit again, by myself. But again nothing happened.

I realized later, of course, that I was still seeking "the gift and not the Giver." I was hoping for an experience to *create* faith in me, instead of yielding my will totally to God, and *in faith* stepping out on "the assurance of things hoped for" (Hebrews 11:1), as Shirley had done.

The change in Shirley was immediate; she now felt she had something to share with others—particularly with her two sisters, Julie and Jenny.

In her long search for reality and a living relationship with God, she had shared her desires with them. Sensitive and responsible as they are, they too, had sensed the vacancy in their lives, that "missing something," even though they went to church. Now, Shirley's assurance that Christ was truly living in her was further heightened by the overflowing love that God gave her for her sisters. Though she didn't give them the whole reason yet, they saw a marvelous change in her.

For almost immediately tragedy struck. This was the sudden death of Red Foley, Shirley's father, in Ft. Wayne, Indiana.

I had always been impressed at how close the Foley family ties were, even when they were separated for long periods of time. They laughed and cried together with unashamed affection, and Shirley loved Red in a deep and tender way. When she called to tell me, I was in Minneapolis—I could

112

Pat & Shirley, his No. 1 fan

Pat and his Grandma Pritchard

Grandpa Pritchard and his boy Pat

His "girls" make a guest appearance on the "Pat Boone Show

Happiness is . . . family fun!

Who said, "the good guys always wear White hats!"
Pat with his famous White buckskins, "trademark."

How do you spell Pat?

Pat trying to borrow money from Jack Benny?

Pat with Maude Amee and Rex Humbard of Cathedral of Tomorrow

Pat with Evangelist Oral Roberts on his TV special

Pat sings before Southern Baptist Convention in Denver - 1970

Pat, Shirley and girls in Japan

Pat and the women in his life

The smile of "A New Song"

just see her stricken with grief and almost incapacitated in her sorrow. But she wasn't!

When I returned home, I was astonished to discover that Shirley was perfectly composed! She flew to Nashville immediately to be with the rest of the family before the funeral. They were all stunned and shaken with grief, and by her own nature Shirley should have been, too, but now she took the lead in consoling the others. Just before the funeral itself, she and her sisters prayed for the presence of the Comforter—and they literally felt His presence with them! Over 3,000 people saw those girls wearing radiant smiles throughout the service—and after!

Were these the emotional Foley sisters, at their Dad's funeral? The next morning, the *Nashville Tennessean* carried Shirley's smiling face on the front page! Certainly the Holy Spirit was with her now in an unusual and remarkable way. Clearly God had turned tragedy into triumph.

Then one evening Satan struck in a vicious way. Though Shirley told only three or four close friends of her meeting with Jesus as Baptizer in the Holy Spirit, the story circulated somehow and became distorted. She received telephone calls from friends who were concerned that she might have had a mental breakdown; others heard she'd been "delivered" from alcoholism!

As she says, when these stories came back to her, she began to question the experience herself, because they made it sound so irrational and exaggerated. This in turn limited her ability to praise God freely and resist the power of Satan.

But God was faithful. Seemingly by accident more and more devout and Spirit-filled people were entering our lives —just when we needed them. Shirley's confidence and faith returned; she began to minister to others.

Very soon, she was invited with her sister Julie to a Bible study in the home of a friend. She had prayerfully asked the Lord in advance whether or not she should tell them about her meeting with the Holy Spirit, since up to this time she had shared it only with four other intimate friends, not including Julie! The answer in the form of a very strong impression appeared to be "yes."

As she approached the subject, however, one young woman excused herself and left—she said she had to go on an errand. Shirley, at first thought this interruption was an indication that she should say no more. But then the hostess asked her point-blank, "Shirley, you've found the Holy Spirit, haven't you?" Shirley discovered that all of those who remained were eager to hear, because *they themselves had been asking the Lord for* a closer relationship with Him. She hadn't known that, and they had no idea what Shirley had to offer! But it seemed to all that God had brought them together, and He knew that the young woman who left abruptly was not prepared. She would have been only a disturbing element in the group.

Julie says that if she'd heard Shirley's story under any other circumstances, she'd have thought her sister had "flipped!" But the eager receptiveness of these intelligent, spiritual women convinced her that this was something for her as well. God is so good, so perfect in His ways. Since then, all of the women of that little group, including Julie, have been baptized in the Holy Spirit.

No sooner had Shirley's father died, than the best friend of our oldest daughter, Cherry, died of a brain tumor. At her funeral, with 200 of their school chums there, we watched Cherry stand in front of the open casket and talk about her 14-year old friend, Wendy. Only months before, Wendy had surrendered her life to Christ. Now Cherry told how the two of them with other Christian friends, had gone down on Sunset Strip and talked about Jesus with the hippies—and of the times she and Wendy had prayed together. While many wept, she concluded by saying that although death had temporarily separated them, nothing could take Wendy from her heart or prevent their being together again someday with their Lord. Two-hundred kids will never forget that afternoon—and neither will we!

Now the Devil started getting *rough!* Shirley was attending a political rally in Long Beach where she had opportunity to share with a dynamic young minister friend of ours, what God had done for her when Red died, and for Cherry at Wendy's funeral. The minister's response was "You've become quite a mystic, Shirley!" Then stooping down, he took the face of our youngest child in his hands and said, "Honey, don't let your momma make a nun of you."

Though he seemed to be half-kidding, the incident shook Shirley to the core. Was it even remotely possible that she'd just been on some satanic mystic "trip"?

She realized then that she had to know for sure that what had happened to her was truly from God, before she could share it further with anybody—and especially with her own children!

Shirley was quiet all the way home, and as we got ready for bed, I noticed she was troubled. When I asked her, she said she didn't want to talk about it. At length, however, she admitted her concern about the conversation with the minister. Then she said, "I don't think I'll pray in my new language any more."

"Honey," I asked, "you aren't going to let the uninformed intellect of one well-meaning young minister rob you of what the Lord Himself has given you, are you?"

But sure enough, it had robbed her temporarily and my "informed" intellect couldn't give it back. Only God could.

CHAPTER 14

I SING A NEW SONG

Shirley was deeply troubled and withdrawn as we got into bed. Nothing I could say seemed to console her, or even reach her.

She had become aware of the cunning of Satan and his own spiritual power to deceive, to counterfeit, to mislead. Like many women today she had often read her horoscope and wondered about the source of these half-truths. The emphasis on mediums, séances, and a whole spiritual world of black magic charms, and even Satan worship is common talk today in social as well as other circles. Shirley needed to be absolutely sure that her experience was based on Bible truth—not on some mystical experience totally outside of God.

In the dark as she was drifting into a troubled sleep, I became aware that she was whispering something to herself.

"What, honey?" I asked. "What are you saying?"

In her drowsy state, she hadn't realized that she'd been mumbling audibly.

"I don't know what I am saying," she replied. "It's just a phrase from my prayer language—I've heard myself saying it over and over."

I listened closely because naturally I was intrigued. I wasn't expecting to understand what she was saying, but suddenly I was transfixed. My wife was praising the Lord— in Latin. I knew she had never had a day of Latin, but I had studied it four years. Yet now she was saying very distinctly, "Ave Deum! Ave Deum! Ave Deum" or *Praise God"* in a language she'd never learned.

When I told her, she began to weep, and immediately knelt by the bed and began truly to praise Her Lord, in a lovely flow of the most beautiful language I've ever heard. In awe, and gratitude, I knelt beside her and thanked God for confirming to both of us, in a way only He could have devised, that this language was truly a gift of His Spirit. Would, or *could,* Satan have caused Shirley to "praise God" in words she'd never learned and *didn't even understand,* except in her spirit? Inconceivable!

We knew we'd just experienced a miracle. The Holy Spirit had given Shirley a phrase that He knew I could interpret, and for our mutual faith and edification.

In the next few days, as if to dispel any idea that this was a coincidence, He made Shirley aware of two other phrases. These, too, were Latin. Aware that our 14-year-old Cherry had studied the language two years, Shirley hesitantly asked Cherry on two separate occasions if the phrases meant anything in Latin.

One was "Te amo dominus," which Cherry immediately knew to mean "I love you, Lord," in Latin!

The other was "Deum amamas," or "We love you, God." Again, Cherry interpreted, with no idea of the source of the phrases. At this point, she knew nothing about a "prayer language."

Can you imagine the joy we felt? Not just because of the three specific phrases themselves—we don't believe Shirley regularly prays in Latin (Why should she?)—but because our all-knowing God chose to confirm to us in this rich way that we *can communicate* our *deepest feelings* to Him in the Holy Spirit! She'd been magnifying God in a language she'd never learned, "as the Spirit gave utterance."

All doubt was gone. Since this incident our lives haven't been the same.

After all, as I've come to realize, what heavenly difference does the language make? God knows our *hearts* and what we need—*before we ask* (Matthew 6:8); it's the love and praise we feel that matters. Paul said so clearly, "If I speak with the *tongues* of *men* and of *angels,* but do not have love, I have become a noisy gong or a clanging cymbal" (I Corinthians 13:1).

Don't get me wrong. I know we should make every effort to express our needs and feelings in our natural language; but how many ways can you think of to tell God you love Him? Paul said clearly in I Corinthians 14:2, "for one who speaks in a tongue does not speak to men but to God; for no one understands, but in his spirit he speaks mysteries." No wonder that the learned apostle recommended praying both "with the spirit" and "with the mind also!" (I Corinthians 14:14,15).

And God gave us another gift that beautiful night. He returned, in rich abundance, the lost love that Shirley felt for *me!* On my part, although I hadn't yet entered into this relationship with the Holy Spirit, I also felt a greater love for Shirley than I had for many months. From that moment until now, love that was dying has continually blossomed into an ever richer and more beautiful relationship. The tender Spirit of the living Lord has given increasing dimension to our love for each other, for our children, and for every other child of God. Now we begin to understand what Paul was saying when he spoke of the "fruit of the Spirit" (Galatians 5:20). "But the fruit of the Spirit is love, joy, peace, patience, kindness, goodness, faithfulness, gentleness, self-control;

119

against such there is no law" (Galatians 5:22-23).

This new capacity for love, as well as the other "fruit of the Spirit" in our daily lives, proves to us even more than the prayer language that Jesus' own Spirit is truly dwelling *in* us. But wait, I'm getting ahead of myself.

Now that God had confirmed *Shirley's* relationship with the Holy Spirit so emphatically—what was holding me?

Incredibly, I was still having a tussle! My mind was still reminding me that traditional Christianity has outgrown emotional display—and especially, the supernatural work of the Holy Spirit in our day. And yet, I also recalled an incident which happened in the lobby of the Manhattan Church of Christ, when we lived in New York City.

After a Sunday evening service, I had heard a young man telling a group of young people how he had set a friend straight. His friend claimed to have "prayed in tongues," but he had told him that he couldn't, that it was wrong, a violation of the Scripture.

"It's impossible—you may have had some psychological release, but that's all!" the young man had insisted.

Although I believed what he was saying was doctrinally correct, and I shared his conviction about it, I had to stop him.

"Wait a minute," I objected. "How can you possibly tell somebody what he has, or has not experienced—when you weren't in his skin at the time? You can tell him what you believe or don't believe. You can tell him what you think the Scriptures say, or what you think they do not say. But to go beyond that is presumptuous—and dangerous."

Judging another's religious experience is always dangerous, as the Pharisees of Jesus' day, and even Paul, found out. But still we do it—and I knew I would be judged. Was I ready?

First, I had met Clint Davidson, seen his life and heard his accounts of miracles in our day.

Then I had read about David Wilkerson and later met him.

120

He not only confirmed Clint's accounts of miracles today, but added the dimension of a prayer language.

My good friend and business associate, George Otis, had added some amazing light on what the Bible actually has to say about the indwelling Holy Spirit and receiving by faith the gifts of the Spirit.

Finally I was seeing my own wife, Shirley, being transformed from a frustrated and confused woman into a beautiful Christian personality—radiating peace and joy, devotion to Jesus, love for me and her girls, a passion for the Bible and a deep concern for others' problems. Her "newness of life" was the most profound testimony of all!

And the others! I was meeting so *many* men and women —usually in Bible studies and in prayer groups—who had met the Holy Spirit and had discovered this exciting new relationship to God! I could just see they'd "been with Jesus," feel in them the power and joy of living the Christian life! It was real!

I couldn't help but contrast them to so many faithful but powerless Christians I knew—so sure they were right, but with little else to share with a drowning world.

I wanted this joy. I needed this power. I longed for this baptism in the Holy Spirit. In fact, I was not only *hoping* it was possible, now I was *believing*.

But what about the old objections? I knew so many.

Objection: not everybody in the early church appears to have been baptized with the Holy Spirit, therefore the experience was not for all, and was not to be perpetuated. But what about Paul's injunction to all Christians in Ephesians 5:18, "And do not get drunk with wine, for that is dissipation, but *be filled with the Spirit*."? This comparison reminded me that on the day of Pentecost (Acts 2), the crowds first thought the apostles had been drinking—but they'd been *filled with the Spirit!* And didn't Peter say that day that the promise of the Holy Spirit was "for *all* who are far off?"

Objection: according to I Corinthians 13:8, "tongues. . .

will cease" because ". . .when the perfect comes, the partial will be done away" (I Corinthians 13:10).

But what does "that which is perfect" mean?

Individual Christians? Hardly; although God's Scriptures "thoroughly furnish" a man so that he "may be perfect" (II Timothy 3:17). I don't know any who've made it, including Paul himself.

The Church? I couldn't accept that proposition. The church had already been established when Paul said that, and it was far from perfect even then, except in its perfect, simple design. And look at it today.

The Bible? This is what most folks think — "that which is perfect" is the Bible, the finished Word of God. But even when it was finished and it *is* perfect, who could obtain it? For 1500 years, few people had access to even a part of God's word. The Gideon Bible in the Hotel room is a recent thing, as is, for that matter, the printing press.

No, it seemed clear to me (as it's worded in some translations of the Bible) that "that which is perfect" refers to the end of God's perfect plan, the completion of His work, or at least the perfect state of things brought about by Christ's return to reign in person, the establishment of "a new heaven and a new earth" (Revelation 21:1). Because only then, as Paul indicated, we shall "see him face to face" and "know *even as we are known*" (Who can claim that now?). And though faith, hope and love "abide now" because we "know in part"; *then,* only "the greatest of these"—love—will remain, when God's perfection is come. Faith and hope will no longer be necessary.

Objection: belief in a "Holy Spirit baptism" separate from water baptism violates Paul's statement to the Ephesians, "There is one body, and one Spirit, just as also you were called in one hope of your calling; one Lord, one faith, *one baptism,* one God and Father of all who is over all and through all and in all" (Ephesians 4:4-6).

And yet the Bible, and Jesus Himself, seemed to speak of *three baptisms*—water, Holy Spirit, and fire! Which *one* was Paul talking about? As I read over that whole fourth chapter of Ephesians, I found Paul crying for "unity in the Spirit" (v. 3), "the Holy Spirit of God, by whom you were sealed for the day of redemption" (v. 30)!

And as I looked at the incredible divisions in Christendom today, caused by the well-intentioned but limited intellects of men—I knew that *only the indwelling Spirit of God could ever unite us!* Jesus prayed so passionately in John 17, "that they may all be one; even as thou, Father, art *in Me,* and I *in Thee,* that they also may be in Us."

How could Jesus be *in* His Father? And His Father *in* Him? Only by the *super-natural living Spirit of God*—and only that supernatural living Spirit *in us* could ever make us all one!

And so, day by day, the intellectual barriers were falling; the time-honored "doctrines," arguments and objections all were melting before Jesus' simple question, "If you then, being evil, know how to give good gifts to your children, how much more shall your Heavenly Father give the Holy Spirit to those who ask Him?" (Luke 11:13).

One last, big question remained: what was this precious relationship going to cost me—in terms of career, reputation, church standing—and even financial security? As if to remind me that I still lived in a real world, Satan immediately hit me below the belt—in my wallet!

As I look back now it's interesting to see the way everything was boiling to a head. At the same time that Shirley was rejoicing in her new-found relationship to Jesus Christ through His Spirit, I was becoming snarled up in the worst financial disaster of my life!

The year before, a partner and I had bought the Oakland basketball team in the newly formed American Basketball Association. I loved the game—and still play amateur basketball five months of the year. It seemed a natural to become involved in the founding of the ABA, and to invest in the Oakland Oaks franchise.

A natural—if you're as rich as John Paul Getty! The

thing began to eat us alive, and because I was busy with personal appearances, keeping a couple of TV shows going, recording and singing and many other things, we decided that my partner would take the majority of stock and run the operation. That first year, 1967, Rick Barry sat out the season, we finished last in the league, and Oakland sports fans treated us like lepers!

So—in addition to my career problems, marital tensions and profound spiritual questions—now total financial disaster threatened.

Though I've always been Mr. Optimist himself, there appeared to be no hope whatever. Everything I tried to do would start out fine, and then fizzle out. Even if there were partial successes in one area, failure cropped up in another. The more I tried to hold my bag of sand together, the more it unravelled. Thank God, I was getting so low there was only one way to look.

Up.

Meanwhile, Shirley had been praying that my eyes would be turned from the material things. In fact, she claims that she was actually praying for temporary failure in my career, and even in business, if that would bring about my total commitment to God, to a deeper spirituality and closer walk with Him. How's that for True Love?

She realized it was my fears and doubts about my career and my whole financial structure that were swamping my thoughts; they were preventing my total surrender, that one-to-one relationship with Jesus that I needed.

I must backtrack for a moment. On September 19th, 1968 I received a frantic call from my accountant about the Oakland Oaks; there had been an incredible overdraft and the bank was demanding $700,000 within 24 hours! I was in Minneapolis for an appearance, but I grabbed the first plane for L.A., my heart in my throat. For some unexplainable reason we were grounded in Las Vegas for an hour. When I called home, Shirley told me that her dad, Red Foley, had just died.

So here we were both slugged between the eyes, shot from ambush, stampeded! Yet, the next day, in spite of her father's death, Shirley didn't need help; in fact, she encouraged me in my desperate efforts to scrape up $700,000 by five o'clock that afternoon!

Our prayers were never more urgent; and miraculously, the Wendell West Real Estate Company with which I'm connected came up with the money *in one day!* Of course, I still was personally faced with the problem of how to pay it back. Moreover, in the month that lay ahead, my advisers did some long overdue checking and discovered I was potentially wiped out. In fact, this news came as I was about to take off for a three-week engagement in Australia. In spite of Superstar Rick Barry and a revitalized team burning up the ABA, we were losing money by the trainload, and the total of my personal involvement now stood at almost $2 million.

That Australian trip found me at the lowest emotional ebb of my whole life. I prayed on the plane all the way down, most of the time I was there, and all the way back.

As the days slipped by and the time drew closer when I might have to come up with the $2 million, the skin began to peel off my fingers. I've never been a nervous type, and I couldn't believe it!

The doctor said, "I'll give you something to put on it, but it's coming from the inside, and nothing you put on the outside is going to help. It's nerves, and you're probably stuck with this for the rest of your life."

At times I could look at my fingers and see what appeared like three or four layers of skin showing. I began to worry that my whole world was falling apart. Where was God? Did he see the agony I was in? Was it all going to end like this?

While I was in Australia, Shirley had to meet with the lawyers and financial advisors. She discussed matters she

125

hardly knew anything about, and amazingly secured signatures that would have been invaluable if everything had caved in.

When I got home, I went for help in two different directions.

With the immense financial problems facing me, I brought in topflight lawyers and financial experts. They worked night and day for a solution.

But, I was coming more and more to the conclusion that although these financial people could help, only God was going to solve the problem. And I knew I couldn't expect Him to solve this problem unless I belonged totally to Him. So now I found myself searching for a closeness to my Father—with a willingness to surrender completely and yield myself to Him. In fact, I began to wonder if maybe I was about to lose my career as an entertainer and embark on some whole new phase of life. I had to have God leading me, wherever I was going.

At last, all the barriers were down.

In January of 1969, I determined that the gift of the Holy Spirit *could* be for me—if I was willing to claim it. That evening I went over to the home of George Otis. By this time I had determined that above everything else, I wanted the Lord in control of my life, and wherever He took me I was willing to go.

So George started with the Old Testament and worked right on through the New Testament.

With our Bibles open we read what the word of God has to say about God, the Holy Spirit and how a man can meet Him through faith. We talked about Peter and how he responded when he saw Jesus walking to him on the water in Matthew 14. He wanted to go to Jesus; but to get there he needed the "gift" of being able to walk on the water, and Peter asked Jesus for it.

Jesus said, "Come." Here was the *promise, the right, the authority.*

Peter didn't wait for some overwhelming power to pick him up and take him to Jesus' side. He knew he had to throw his legs over the side of that boat and step out on the slapping waves. So he did. The result was—he found himself *walking on the water* toward the Lord! The trouble came when he took his eyes off Jesus, when he looked around at the waves and said, "Wait a minute, this can't be happening. . .!"

And sure enough it wasn't. Jesus had to haul him out of the water, saying "O you of little faith, why did you doubt?" (Matthew 14:31).

I believed this thrilling story; and right then I wanted, just like Peter *to go to* Jesus. I knew I had the promise and the right. But faith had to take over; I had to "throw my legs over the side" and give myself to Him—my brain, my personality, my voice—everything. Then I must have the faith to believe that what occured then was the Lord's will, and thank Him for it.

The moment had come. George and I were alone in the room. We raised our arms to God, and I prayed. "O Father, this is it—I give up. I yield my life to You. Please take it, Lord, and make of it whatever You want to. Forgive me of every sin, wash me clean; and Jesus, Oh, precious Jesus , be my baptizer. *Baptize me right now* in Your Spirit, the Spirit of the living God."

Even as I prayed I began to sense the Lord's presense in a remarkable way. I began by simply offering my voice to Jesus and supporting a tone. As I did, *a beautiful melody came out,* and words began to float in on the melody! It was such a graceful and beautiful thing that I hardly recognized the voice as mine. And a warmth, an assurance filled my spirit.

How can I describe such a thing? It was an uplifting, inspiring, joyful experience—the most profound of my life. I had a deep sense of knowing that I was *singing a new song to God.*

My baptism was so different from Shirley's; but then, *she*

and I are so different. And Jesus is so graceful, so personal. Where Shirley prayed in an expressive, spoken language, alone, for 45 minutes—I sang a lovely, quiet song, full of gratitude and love. Jesus, *in us,* allowed us to still be ourselves!

Maybe this is why there's absolutely no description of the individual baptisms in the New Testament—precisely because they *were* so individual!

Since then I also praise the Lord in a prayer language as well; but singing in the Spirit is especially precious to me.

Like anything else, the more I've exercised my gift, the more expressive it has become in pouring out adoration, love, gratitude—and so often, my need—to God. Whatever my spiritual feelings are—when I run out of English and find myself groping self-consciously for the way to express myself—now I find complete freedom as the Holy Spirit, in this unfettered, infinitely expressive prayer language helps me to communicate directly with my Heavenly Father through Jesus Christ my Lord.

Isn't this the whole purpose of prayer? Jesus said, "Your Heavenly Father knows what you need *before you ask,"* and Paul claims the Holy Spirit Himself "intercedes for us with groanings too deep for words which cannot be uttered" (Romans 8:26).

Which of us can even be sure that he expresses himself adequately in normal conversation? I can't. So how can we hope to express how we feel, or what we need, when we pray to God? He's given us a prayer language as an individual means of communication! No wonder Paul says, "One who speaks in tongues *edifies himself"* (I Corinthians 14:4).

The most thrilling part of all is the realization that the God of the Universe has drawn intimately close to *me* and has given *me* a gift from His Spirit, a gift that confirms to me everything I ever believed—or tried to believe—about God in the past. In this regard the Bible says, "The Spirit Himself *bears witness* with our spirit that we are children of

God" (Romans 8:16).

Man, that good Bible reads like today's newspaper now! It's not 2,000, or 4,000 years old now—it's today! God hasn't changed; and things that seemed uninteresting, distant, irrelevant or confusing before jump to life and meaning as His Spirit helps me to understand. It's great!

I was astonished to see how many times the Holy Spirit is mentioned in the New Testament. All the writers—whether they were prophets or apostles—were so intimately involved with the Holy Spirit that they gave Him credit for everything. I couldn't help remembering how Jesus talked to Nicodemus about the Holy Spirit in John 3. He compared Him to the wind, and He said that nobody knows where the wind comes from or where it goes, but all can see the signs of its blowing. That tells me that when we start trying to put limits on our understanding of the Holy Spirit and contain Him in any way, we are violating what Jesus said. Instead we must realize that the Spirit of God is moving in ways *God* chooses —not how or where or when *we* have decided He should move.

What? The Oakland Oaks problem? Oh, I'll finish that story shortly; it's fantastic! But first, something infinitely more important.

CHAPTER 15

A NEW FAMILY RELATIONSHIP

The other day the newspaper told about an attractive 15-year-old girl who, quite unexpectedly, had left home a year before.

To the newspaper reporters, her parents described their home life as "happy." They had assumed Pam enjoyed riding her horse, playing with her dogs, and entertaining her friends at parties.

But one morning they found a note in her room. She said she wanted to "find out about the world." So she had left home.

From time to time her frantic parents had heard of her whereabouts from rumors or tips from her friends. But whenever they tried to track her down, she disappeared.

According to the newspaper report, her body was found in a hippie pad in a distant city. She was seven months pregnant, and had died of an overdose of narcotics.

Don't you read stories like this in *your* newspaper, almost every day now? And doesn't it impress you that, in a startling percentage of these tragedies, the kids involved come from average, middle class, "happy" homes?

Living in the community of Beverly Hills, Shirley and I have seen this happen again and again. And for so long, we sensed how uncertain *our own* family relationships were. Knowing we'd soon be the parents of four teen-age girls we were deeply concerned. What would *their* future be?

They weren't dummies; they'd felt the tensions building up between Shirley and me. What hope could they have that their family life would be any different from ours?

Then Shirley and I fell in love all over again: with each other, with our children, with God after He filled us with His Holy Spirit. Now our love for each other transcended anything we had ever known before—not because of anything *we* had achieved, as individuals—but because Jesus, as He promised, was living *in* us in growing measure. And we'd told the girls, as best we could, the reason for our transformation.

But could we expect to see the Holy Spirit work the same miracle in the lives of our four children—Cherry 15, Lindy 14, Debbie 13, and Laury 12? Naturally, we'd prayed for them since they were babies.

In the days to come, we were to witness *the most amazing demonstration* of God's answers to a parent's prayers.

It all began one evening when Shirley and I were home alone with Laury. We had meant to go out someplace, but for trivial, frustrating reasons, the plans had fallen through. Meanwhile, the three older girls had gone out to parties or to spend the night at friends' homes.

As I recall it, I was feeling definitely hacked; no movie, and with half of the troops gone, we couldn't enjoy a "family night," either. Usually Laury would just kidnap the TV set and "tune out" till bedtime.

Besides, Laury, as the youngest, had been our "problem child." She's a muscular, energetic, an impulsive little dynamo. She's never been interested in school, and she

132

continually got into trouble. She'd do whatever she'd think of, almost in the same instant that she'd think of it. Sort of like a monkey.

More than with any of the others, we would fuss at her.

"Laury, why did you do that? We've told you a thousand times *not* to!"

And her reply usually was the same.

"I don't know. I forgot."

Like the time a couple of years ago when she absent-mindedly scratched her initials in a floral design on the surface of the piano in the living room. They couldn't be removed or filled in, in fact, they're still there.

This happened just a few days before Christmas! But we decided, that she had to be punished anyway; we had to teach her that she couldn't always follow her "artistic" impulses. So, "Santa changed his mind" about her big red bicycle. It was the only thing she'd asked for. Instead, Christmas morning, she found a note in her stocking from "Santa" saying, "Laury, I love you, but I know about the piano, and I can't give you the bicycle I had picked out for you. If you'll try a little harder, you can have it next Christmas."

You think that wasn't rough on a Mom and Dad, too?

Her eyes filled with tears then she smiled and said, "He's right; I'll just wait."

Now *our* eyes filled with tears.

A month later, we gave the bicycle to her for her birthday.

That lesson appeared to help, for a while. But others had to follow to encourage her to discipline herself. I've often thought of her as being like Peter, the apostle of Jesus. He was quick on the trigger, good-hearted, but often wrong. He took out his sword and chopped off a soldier's ear one night. Jesus put the ear back on and said, "Put your sword away."

It was Peter too, the only one in the whole boat load of

men, who jumped out and walked on the water to meet Jesus. Laury is just that impulsive. She sees something or thinks of something, and she wants to do it immediately!

On this particular evening, we thought she was watching television in her room. Instead, she'd been reading her Bible and praying. She had told Shirley a lie earlier that day and wanted to confess it. Now she came down to tell us. As we talked with her she said, "I really do want to be more like Jesus. But it's so hard. Do you think it would help if I asked Him to baptize me in His Spirit like you and Mommy?"

At first I'll admit it was difficult for me to believe that this was for real. Here was our little maverick saying "Can I ask the Lord to take over in my life, and maybe give me a prayer language like you have?" We just weren't ready for that!

Up to this point, Shirley and I hadn't talked much about it or how we could help our children enter into this relationship with the Holy Spirit. If we had, obviously we would have started with Cherry, the oldest and worked down to Laury. But now that she, as the youngest, was the first to ask, we couldn't refuse to pray with her. We were more astonished when, as we prayed together, the Holy Spirit quickly answered and she began to worship her Lord in a prayer language!

Try to imagine the thrill we felt, as parents, that glorious evening!

Looking back over it now, I can see God's infinite wisdom. He chose her first, partly because she was the first one to come and ask Him, in her own impulsive way. But there was something else, very vital and precious. Laury has always been sort of an outcast, so far as the other girls were concerned. They loved her, and yet she is the youngest, and has been slower to mature both emotionally and intellectually. She was still "the baby." Whenever she said something she thought was funny, or tried to chime in on the conversation, the other girls would chorus:

"Oh, Laury, forget it."

But God says that He chooses the foolish things to confound the wise. He took the stone the builders rejected, and made it the cornerstone of our faith. (This, of course, refers to Jesus the carpenter's son, our Christ and Messiah.) And I believe this is why He chose little Laury—because we'd have been too wise to do it.

The other girls were first surprised, and then a little suspicious. But there was no denying the reality of Laury's experience with the Holy Spirit. The change in her life became apparent immediately to all of us. She demonstrated a new dimension of love for us all, and clearly evidenced a. new desire to please her Lord, now so near to her.

It was as though the Lord was saying to us, "You've been looking at Laury's imperfections. But I have accepted her. Maybe she was the least in your eyes, but she is special in Mine; she has as much right to My Holy Spirit as any of you."

With Laury's blazing new life in the Spirit, it was obvious to Shirley and me that the others would soon desire to have the same relationship.

Cherry came next. She has a very high IQ, is very creative and mature for her years. As I write this she is only 15 but appears more like 19. Older boys have always been attracted to her. She possesses unusually good judgment and has a great sense of humor. She's well disciplined, and yet her emotions surface quickly.

Because Cherry is a deep thinker, she could see that what the Holy Spirit had done first for Shirley and me, and then for Laury, was valid and real. But because she was the oldest child, she had imbibed more deeply of the doctrines of the church, and hence had more to consider than the others.

However, events had prepared her in an unusual way for accepting the reality of the Holy Spirit. She became mysteriously ill. Exhausted by the pressure of schoolwork, she suffered from frequent nosebleeds, and a serious swelling developed around her eyes. I was out of town, and Shirley was about to call the doctor. But she felt led first to ask George Otis to join her in praying for Cherry.

When George came, he pointed out that he was convinced they should both pray for Cherry, and also anoint her with oil as the Bible gives the instruction. (James 5:14, "Is any sick among you? Let him call for the elders of the church; and let them pray over him, anointing him with oil in the name of the Lord.")

This was Beverly Hills, 1969, and George is an electronics executive but also an elder in the church! But this was something Cherry had not heard of before, so she was somewhat reluctant. Yet as Shirley and George Otis prayed, Cherry *was healed completely of her illness!* It was a startling demonstration that there were new things for her to learn in her walk with the Lord.

Then, several nights later, after praying with a group of Shirley's friends, Cherry came to her mother's bedroom.

"Mommy, did you know that Jesus baptized me with the Holy Spirit tonight, and that I now have a prayer language?" Cherry asked.

"Yes, I had the feeling it had happened," Shirley replied.

"But why didn't you say something about it?"

Shirley explained to Cherry that her experiences were between herself and God, not necessarily with other people. Therefore she felt it was important that Cherry tell us about it only when and if she wanted to! See the freedom in that, even within a family? This counsel proved wise. Because of her own calm and reflective nature, Cherry has continued this relationship with her heavenly Father. She prays in the Spirit continually, but always quietly. And when others may raise their voices in prayer, she buries her head in her arms and simply retires from the group in fellowship with her Lord.

I'd like to share something with you, an example of Cherry's devotion, as well as her creative spirit. At a time when she was spiritually low, the Lord gave her a song which she has put to music. She now accompanies herself on the guitar, and the words go like this.

Father God

Father God, why hast Thou forsaken me?
Can You really see me here-or do You even care?
Father God, if Your love is full and free,
Please take away the pain I feel;
Deliver me from fear.
Father God, the empty words ring loud and clear.
If You're really there, O God, why don't you answer me?
Father God, this world has such a bitter taste;
Is this pain the price that one has to pay?
Time goes by; I ask, and yet I don't receive.
Is it just coincidence that You don't hear me?
Am I dead—or is it You that's gone away?
Where are You now? I need You so—
Is there nothing You can say?

(God's Answer)

Whether you doubt, My child, I love you anyway;
This hell you lived is Satan's kind.
Continue searching—you shall find.
My Son was slain, and rose again from where He lay.
The death you've died is done, so *rise*—'tis your
    resurrection day.

Lindy was the next whom Jesus baptized with the Holy Spirit. She's our second oldest. Of the four, I'd call her the quietest, even more than Debby, who is eleven months younger. The two have many things in common; they share the same room, confide their own secrets.

Lindy has dark hair, eyes, complexion. She's always been the softest spoken, more introspective than the others. And yet I don't think of her as being complex; she's direct rather than devious. We've always felt that she was extremely trustworthy. She's much more likely to behave the same when Mom and Dad aren't around—as when she's with us.

137

This may be because she's more afraid of the consequences of wrong behavior than any of the others, but basically, she's just good.

Lindy is stolid, conscientious about her work; when she has a job to do, she does it painstakingly. Yet, she, too, had to learn that a closer relationship with the Lord does not come easily.

A year ago our German Shepherd dog, Heidi, had a litter of pups. On Lindy's 13th birthday, we gave one of these to Lindy for her own. She named it Shep, after a song which her grandfather, Red Foley, had made famous. Naturally, she became very attached to Shep; and strangely, in her own mind, she said to herself that the only thing which could make her doubt God would be if anything happened to her pal, Shep.

Several days after this, Shep knocked a slat out of the gate and got out into the street in front of our house where he was hit by a car. The neighbors called, and Shirley and her sister, who was visiting us at the time, ran out to the street with the girls.

It was obvious immediately that Shep was dying; and while Lindy was stunned, Debby was the one who needed help. She'd fallen to the ground and was sobbing—mostly because of the grief she knew Lindy was feeling, but also over her own shock in seeing the dog writhing in final agony. The women and girls dropped to their knees with her and began to pray right in our front yard.

I went out to the street in the stalled traffic to see about the dog. At that moment a sightseeing bus, full of tourists from everywhere, stopped to watch and saw Shirley praying with the tearful little group, asking God to be very near, and to cause good to come from even this sorrow. Those tourists probably will never forget that scene.

Lindy pondered this for days, remembering what she'd thought privately about doubting God and decided that somehow, *through* the very thing she dreaded, He'd become, even more real.

Because she is so methodical and logical in her approach to life, Lindy was not sure that the baptism in the Holy Spirit was what God had for her. She knew that both Laury and Cherry had met God in this dimension, and that they were able to worship Him in a more satisfying way through their prayer language. But as yet, she couldn't quite imagine this happening to her.

Meanwhile John Day, the proprietor of the Valley Book and Bible Store, had come to visit. As they were talking afterwards, he turned to Lindy and said, evidently voicing a word of knowledge.

"You're going to be baptized in the Spirit today. As a matter of fact, *it will be around 9:00 tonight.*" And he left. Later we realized he had manifested one of the gifts of the Holy Spirit listed in I Corinthians 12:8.

Inwardly Shirley recoiled at this statement. She knew how unemotional Lindy was, and how suspicious she could become when she thought pressure was being applied. Shirley was fearful that Lindy would react negatively to Day's assertion.

Later on, Lindy admitted that as the time for our nightly prayer session drew closer, she became resistant. She didn't want to be shoved, and as the pressure built up, she dreaded the possibility that something would happen to her at 9:00 that night over which she herself had no control.

We began our session around 8:30 that evening, and one by one we prayed about people and things that concerned us, bringing them before the Lord. Meanwhile, Lindy was arriving at her personal rendezvous with God—not wanting to be coerced into doing something she didn't quite feel ready for—yet at the same time really hungering for a closer relationship to Him. Finally, very gently, as one after another of us began to pray in the Spirit, naturally and quietly *Lindy joined us* in the prayer language which the Lord gave her.

Like both Laury and Cherry's experience, Lindy's also was a natural surrender of her life and personality to God. As Jesus Christ baptized her in His Spirit, she simply lifted her heart to Him in worship and praise and adoration, in a new and wonderful language.

This now meant that Debby, our blonde and next-to-the-youngest, was the only one who had not yet entered into this relationship with the Lord.

Shirley believes that Debby actually was ready to receive her baptism in the Spirit the same evening as Lindy. But because she wanted to *know* that this experience was hers alone, and that she wasn't just being swept along in the emotion of Lindy's baptism, she hung back from full surrender. She was a little like the others in the boat with Peter, who also could have shared Jesus' invitation but for lack of faith and desire.

Of all our four girls, Debby is most likely to have a self-critical attitude and something of an inferiority complex. This may have come from trying to measure up to her two older sisters. Cherry and Lindy both played the piano easily. For Debby it's been harder. While Cherry was a straight "A" student, and Lindy a good "A-B" student, Debbie was more likely to be a "B-C" student. Consequently this may have subconsciously given her the feeling that she wasn't as good as the other girls.

I don't know why, but of the four I would say that Debby is the most thoroughly feminine. She's blue-eyed, fair, and as a little girl always walked around on her tiptoes. She has always known she was a girl. I mean, it was seven or eight years before the other girls realized there was a *difference* between them and the boys they were playing with! Not Debby.

We were particularly eager to see Debby come into her full relationship with Jesus because we know that all of our girls need this inner protection of the Holy Spirit in the turbulent world facing young people today. As I'm saying

140

so often, "You can't isolate kids today, but God can insulate them." At the same time, Shirley was sensing that God was going to use someone else as the catalyst. She didn't know who, and only reluctantly did she submit to the idea.

Then one day Lucinda, our former cook, became ill. I was out of town, and Shirley called George Otis to ask him to come over and pray for her, which he did.

As George was leaving Shirley said, "If you have time, I would appreciate your praying with Debbie. I believe she's ready to be baptized in the Spirit, but I think she needs to talk to someone else besides Pat or me."

As George has recounted it since then, Debby appeared to be under real bondage of the fear of rejection, of being unwanted. She believed that God desired everyone to be baptized in the Spirit, but she lacked the confidence to step out as an individual, and accept what He was offering to her. She was like the little boy on the diving board. He sees his older brother and sister having fun and wants to join them. But he hesitates. He knows there's nothing to fear, and still he's afraid. When he finally takes the step of plunging in, he's surprised at how simple and easy it was.

So George and Debby went out to the little office-guest room behind our house. There they turned to the Word of God, and reviewed what God has to say about the baptism by Jesus Christ which enables a believer in Him to receive the power of the Holy Spirit.

George knew somehow that Debby needed to be reassured that God indeed had authorized *her* baptism in the logic of His Word. She had seen the beautiful changes in each of her sisters. So there was no doubt in her mind about the reality of the Spirit. But did God's Word promise His Spirit to Debby Boone?

Step by step, they went through the Scriptures until she was personally satisfied that this relationship to Jesus Christ could truly be hers. Then they began to pray. Moments later, Otis returned to the house and motioned Shirley to follow him. When she arrived at the office door, Shirley could see Debby calmly seated in a chair worshipping the Lord, tears streaming down her cheeks, radiant with the evidence of His presence and pouring out her heart to Him in a beautiful prayer language.

In many ways, I believe Debby's experience was similar to mine. I really get choked up, remembering the times when we prayed in our family circle for Debby. I can still hear her whispering urgently, "Please, Jesus. Oh, please, Jesus."

And I can hear myself back in those hotel rooms around the country during the months when I was asking the Lord in my desperation to bless me with His Spirit, to give me a prayer language. I always felt rejected afterwards. My problem was that I didn't take the step of faith myself. I asked the Lord to do it all, like the boy on the diving board, instead of Peter on the water.

But, now that each of us has entered into this new and deeper relationship with God through the Holy Spirit, our family life has taken on an enormously exciting dimension. Each of us has a greater sense of his own *individuality* with God. We're bound together as a family, but each of us feels a special, singular identity. We love each other so much more, and yet are more quietly independent than ever, more self-confident.

Debby's growing confidence in herself has been something to see!

One of the first confirmations of this came when we returned several months ago from Japan. I had taken the girls with me on a singing tour during the Easter holidays, and we returned almost a week late for their school. Debby knew she had missed a test, and was going to have to make it up immediately after she returned. She had studied for it, but the old fear of failure loomed up, and the night we got back she came to me.

"Daddy, I'm not ready to take that test. Will you write a note for me and ask my teacher to let me have until next week?"

"I can't, Debby. You've had your book with you, and I know you've studied."

"But Daddy, I'll flunk," she objected.

"Now, wait a minute," I said. "We've been through this before, but now you've got something extra. You have the Holy Spirit to help you, and you know He will."

I went out of town immediately, and was gone two or three days. When I returned, I had forgotten the incident until Debby brought it up at the dinner table. She was wearing a very serious "I told you so" look.

"Daddy, you know that test *you made me take?* The teacher wouldn't let me put it off, and you said to *pray* about it?"

"Yeh," I said, almost bracing myself for the worst.

"I made an 'A'," she said.

I was dumb-struck, and we all howled at my reaction. Then we stopped immediately to thank the Lord for the way in which He had helped Debby.

With each of the girls, God has known the wisest and best way to confirm His reality to them.

Little Laury is still just as impulsive and rambunctious as ever. But now she's quicker to realize that she's made a mistake and to correct her actions.

Before she was filled with the Holy Spirit, she kept getting out of line at school. Each report card appeared to be a little worse than the previous one.

The straw that broke the camel's back came when one of her friends at school was put in isolation as punishment for perpetual disobedience. She was confined in a room by herself to spend the day studying and working on assignments. No one was allowed to come and see her, but several times, Laury "forgot," and sneaked in to console her friend. Eventually Laury was caught and put on probation herself.

Today, this sort of defiance is virtually all in the past. Her grades are up. She's stopped blindly running with the friends who were always getting into trouble. Now she knows that the Holy Spirit is with her, *in* her, and not simply at home with Mama and Daddy. He's become a constant companion to her, and she knows she's accountable to Him, even more than to us. And He's too precious to lose!

So it's been with the other girls as well. It's been fascinating to see how the Spirit of God has moved through them. They possess the same personalities, but the Holy Spirit has adapted His method of operation to those personalities, enriching them and enlarging them in their outreach to their friends.

The knowledge and awareness of the Holy Spirit in their lives is causing the good qualities to rise to the top and the flaws and bad habits (our failures, probably), whatever they might be, to filter down to where they're less significant.

Since our walk in the Spirit began, we've had some unsuccessful family prayer times. This has happened when one of the girls was at odds with another. The result was a worrying or troubling affect on us all. We knew something was wrong, but we didn't know what to do about it. I can't say these incidents have disappeared completely; but I do know that the Holy Spirit has enabled the girls more quickly to identify their hang-ups, admit them and ask forgiveness — of both one another and of God. The results have been an altogether new and refreshing sense of God's presence and love in our family relationships.

Meanwhile, many of our friends say that they've seen a remarkable change in the way the girls *look!* To them, they appear brighter, perhaps more alert and maybe in some ways more feminine and attractive. I don't know (I can't be objective), but I will have to admit that almost overnight an increasing number of young people appear to be attracted to them and to our home. These young people come from the homes of entertainment personalities and business and professional executives in our community. Boys and girls, they come, apparently because they've seen something

144

different in the lives of our girls. And because what they've seen has been alive and vibrant, and because the girls talk so openly about their friend Jesus, a large number of their friends have come to know Him too!

All of our girls have been offered pills and marijuana at school ("You can't isolate kids."). But each of them has *told us* when this has happened. And immediately, each has made the person who offered her the drugs the subject of special prayer (sometimes with heartwarming results). The same has happened when their schoolfriends have reported illnesses or alcoholic or domestic problems at home. Their "Christian club" has grown rapidly.

Today, besides praying for their friends here in our prayer circle, the girls in the club have found a wooded place on their schoolgrounds where they meet to pray. Cherry tells me there's hardly an hour of the day when there aren't two or three of the girls meeting in this secluded spot to pray for the conversion of someone, a special problem, or almost anything in connection with their home or school life. They've found out God *does* care!

Of course, we keep all these things to ourselves. We don't pressure these young folks when they come to our home. We don't fly off the handle or become "stool pigeons," reporting incidents of dope peddling to school authorities. We haven't had to, for we've watched God bring so many of these confused searching young people into His fold, and I've had the thrilling satisfaction of baptizing them in our swimming pool when they have personally committed their lives to Jesus Christ.

The other day, for instance, I got permission from the school principal to pick up a couple of girls at the lunch period and bring them home. Our girls reported that these two dear friends, Ellen and Merrilee, had given their lives to Christ as their Savior, and now wanted to be baptized. It was a warm sunny day, and after I heard their confession of faith I baptized them in the shallow end of the pool. The

145

sun itself was no brighter than the radiance in those two wet, beautiful young faces!

In fact, I suppose there are more than twenty of these girls who have come to know Jesus in the last year. Many of them have come from homes of famous parents who haven't had time for religion. And interestingly enough, some of these parents are now starting to wonder just what it is that's caused such happy changes in their kids.

One girl was telling me the other evening that her mother, a well-known actress who is estranged from her husband, asked about the Bible.

"Tell me all you know about it. Maybe God can do for me what He's done for you," the actress said to her daughter.

Meanwhile, the daughter has written her father urging him to pray for the Lord's guidance in his life. Isn't that wonderful? We praise God!

In another home, the parents have decided that they need more of what they've seen in their son's life. The wife called Shirley and asked if she and her husband might come over and sit in on the Bible studies we're having so often in our home.

It hasn't all been roses, of course. One of the "new girls" is Jewish! The 15-year-old girl accepted Christ as her Savior and was baptized in our swimming pool. Her radiant life and testimony since then has become so disturbing to her parents that they first sent her to one of the best known rabbis in the Los Angeles area. To my amazement, he ridiculed her faith in Jesus Christ, told her he knows the Evangelist Billy Graham, whom he claimed "doesn't believe, himself, most of what he preaches," and rather mockingly advised her to give up "this silly Jesus business."

When the 15-year-old girl failed to recant, she was sent to a psychiatrist. After extended visits, he told her there was absolutely nothing wrong with her. Then he astonished her by adding, "Honey, you're a good Christian!"

Meanwhile, the parents have temporarily forbidden their

146

daughter to come to our home. They've taken away her New Testament, and in many other ways restricted her because of her faith in Christ. What confuses and agitates them most of all is their daughter's calm and persistent *love for them,* in the face of their frantic efforts to convince her she's made a mistake.

We know the heartbreak and confusion they're going through. We imagine sometimes how we'd feel if the situation were reversed. So we're praying fervently that Jesus will speak so eloquently through the changed lives of these Beverly Hills kids that soon each of these parents will want to meet and thank Him!

CHAPTER 16

ALL — AND EVERYTHING

Meanwhile, back to the Oakland Oaks. Believe it or not that problem was getting worse everyday while our spiritual lives were just beginning. The old Devil was "gonna do us in," if he could!

I looked at my fingers, around June of 1969 and that *peeling condition was* gone! Here the bank was about to ask me for 2 1/2 million bucks, which I didn't have, and I was getting over that nerve condition completely. My friends thought I was nuts, but Paul's statement in Romans 8:28 "And we know that God causes all things to work together for good to those who love God, to those who are called according to His purpose," was now my theme song. After all, the guy that wrote that had been shipwrecked, beaten, jailed, stoned, left for dead—and was eventually beheaded! And yet he said, "I count it all joy!"

I was just starting to find out what he meant.

The burden of maintaining a career and providing for my family was still there, but I was remembering Jesus' promise,

"But seek first His kingdom, and His righteousness; and all these things shall be added to you" (Matthew 6:33). I was believing Him now and starting to make decisions accordingly! The results have been just incredible.

As a very recent example, moments ago my manager phoned to say that Johnny Carson wanted me to come to New York City and host his Tonight Show while he's out of town. A year or two ago I would have dropped everything and caught a plane immediately. It's fun, and potentially "good for business."

"How will it affect my career if I don't?" would have been my reasoning.

Not so now. I had asked God's will about doing this book. All the indications have been very positive, even to being able to carve out the necessary time. But a busy week in New York City would have seriously delayed my writing, so I had to "pass" on Johnny's offer. I hope he'll invite me again, but for now, I believe God wants this pencil in my hand.

Thank the Lord, I know I'm not at the mercy of anybody or anything! If God can give me a prayer language, and transform my wife and kids before my eyes, He's also able to keep all the other promises I find in the Bible. I'm on the winning team! My responsibility is to read the Word of God, find out what it says, and then by faith, believe and *act upon* what He promised!

I know that sounds more simple than it is. But it is more simple than most of us think! It's as simple as finding out what our rights and promises are, as God's children, and then just depending on Him to work with us and do it! But it's a growth process, too; a series of lessons.

It's almost like playing poker with a stacked deck. We put our whole little stack of chips on one of God's promises; that's the "gamble" of faith. When we win that hand, we keep on playing, and God may increase the stakes as our faith grows. Often we have to risk *all our chips* to win

150

the larger hand, but if it's to the ultimate glory of God, we'll win! Although we'll misplay a few hands now and then, when we don't read our cards right, *God's running the game.* If we don't cheat, get piggish, or start making up our own rules we'll always come away winning! The Lord said, "You were faithful with a few things, I will put you in charge of many things" (Matthew 25:21).

I like playing in a game, even if it's rough *when I know I'm gonna win!*

My confidence in the Spirit's guiding presence grew quickly after my baptism; hope and joy and love branched out in every direction, enfolding everybody I could think of, even that dreaded banker! I woke up smiling in the morning, often saying, "Good morning, Jesus!"

Shirley and I were praying often, about many things, and the startling and specific answers caused our faith to grow. The Lord was real; we felt His presence often, and talked to Him as our friend.

But, though I believed the Lord was *big enough* to solve my Oakland Oaks problem, it took some smaller tests to build my faith that He'd actually *do* it! One of the most dramatic was that of Tetragrammaton.

My contract with Dot Records had expired at the end of 1968 after 13 years. Early in 1969 my manager conferred with several recording companies who wanted me. One was an aggressive new company with owner-partners like Bill Cosby and his manager, Roy Silver; they called it Tetragrammaton. They offered me the best deal I'd ever had. In fact, it was the best deal I ever heard of! So I quickly committed myself to them verbally in the early part of the year.

The terms of the contract had been worked out and now I was about to sign; I had already recorded an album, which was to be my first on the new label. I was in high gear, rarin' to go and trying to ignore a couple of dangerous signs.

One: this was the company that was just then distributing

151

"Two Virgins," the controversial "non-music" LP with the nude pictures of Beatle John Lennon and Yoko Ono on the front and back covers.

At the time I had reasoned, "That's got nothing to do with me. My records won't be like that." I tried not to imagine my album along side "Two Virgins" on the same record rack.

Two: I hadn't really asked the Lord whether I should go with this recording company or not. My impulse was to get the career moving. In fact, I hadn't even told Shirley what I planned to do.

Well, a couple of days before contract signing, George Otis called to say, "Flying back from Virginia the other day I had the strongest impression that I should get you together with a good friend of mine by the name of Harald Bredesen."

He went on to explain that Bredesen was a very unusual and courageous preacher who ministered to the historic First Reformed Church congregation in Mt. Vernon, New York. He was often sent by the Holy Spirit on missions all over the world, often to help prominent people. I'd heard of him and said, "Fine."

I described our meeting and soul-shaking prayer session in the first chapter. You'll remember it was Harald who asked "Are you willing to die to your career?" I'd said I was, if God wanted me to. And the very next day, God put me to the test. It was the day I was to sign the Tetragrammaton contract.

Ten minutes before I was to leave the house, Otis and Bredesen drove up. When I explained where I was going and why, both men seemed troubled although neither had known about the contract before.

"I think we should pray about this before you sign," Otis said.

And Bredesen added, "I think I have a Scripture verse for you." And he quoted II Corinthians 6:14, "Be ye not un-equally yoked together with unbelievers." You can imagine,

152

I was stunned and inwardly a little ticked off!

"It's no skin off their nose if I don't sign," I thought, "but it's bread and butter for me."

And besides, I saw a rejuvenated record career as a big key to the Oakland Oaks solution.

Then I realized that their reaction was spontaneous; they couldn't have any personal motive. Moreover, they were more experienced Christians than I. Also, Bredesen's stabbing question of the night before was still echoing: "Are you willing to die to your career, if this is what God wants?" And I was suddenly afraid that God had heard my answer!

"At least," I thought, "I shouldn't rush out and sign this thing without praying about it."

So I called Tetragrammaton and my manager was already there. "Jack, something has come up, and I just can't come down there today. I'll check with you in the morning," I said. Jack went numb, but agreed.

At home we began to talk and pray about the contract. Both Otis and Bredesen said, "We don't know why we have this strong feeling, Pat. There must be something we don't know, that God is trying to tell us."

Then I confessed that I had been disturbed about several aspects of the situation (neither of which Bill Cosby had anything to do with; he left the running of the company to others). One was the nude album cover on Tetragramma's other new record. Another was some advance advertising on my first record I'd just accidentally heard about—an advertising blurb that was to appear in the trade papers. It read, "Pat Boone sings his ass off."

I explained that after my initial shock, I'd been so hungry for a hit record that I'd rationalized, "I wasn't supposed to know about this; if I hadn't stumbled on it, I wouldn't have known until the ad was printed, and maybe this is just what my career needs. This is bold and different. At least people won't say, Ho hum! Just another Pat Boone record."

It was no longer a mystery to any of us that God had

153

waved a red flag!

A little later Jack called. When he heard of my concerns and the possibility that I might not sign the contract he nearly passed out! Because the Oakland Oaks bills were rivaling the national debt, he knew how much I needed the revenues, and how profitable this contract might prove to be. Royalty was based on a graduate scale, and on a hit record or album it topped out at 14 per cent—an almost unheard of figure!

Quickly we called our lawyers. They warned that since I'd already made a verbal commitment, which had been announced in the trade papers, that I could not walk away from it. *It was binding.* Then I realized, "I'm a Christian. I don't want to back off on commitments I've made. But here I am with a commitment on one hand and a warning from God not to be "unequally yoked" on the other. What am I supposed to do?"

George and Harold were sympathetic but firm—and strangely excited.

"Pat," Harold asked, "Just last night, you said to God that if you knew your own heart, you were willing to die to your career—didn't you?" I nodded.

"Well, here, the very next day, God is giving you a chance to know your own heart! Suppose, you are sued and go bankrupt. What a testimony! Here's one man in the entertainment industry who would rather go bankrupt than deny his Lord!"

I felt like saying, "Hey, this is my career you're scrapping!" But quickly, I knew that they each would put his own career on the line, if he were faced with a similar decision. They only wanted me to be brave enough to do God's will.

But what was it?

I put off the contract meeting two more days—until 3 p.m. the third day. During those two days, I agonized, talked with close friends, searched the Bible and prayed. The last night I took my problem to bed with me. Naturally, I couldn't sleep.

Around midnight, I kissed Shirley and told her I had to go back to that hilltop; she hugged me and said she'd be praying at home. She understood. After throwing on my clothes, I drove through a misting rain to the top of Coldwater Canyon to be alone with God.

He was there.

As I simply talked to Him, walking in circles and pouring out my need and my utter dependence on Him, I knew He was listening. After an hour or more, the midst stopped swirling and I stood still, eyes closed, empty, waiting.

The moment was so silent, so void of motion that everything seemed suspended. And in that moment, a peace and confidence enveloped me; I felt what seemed a reassuring caress—a warm pressure—on my left cheek. And that was all.

Oh, but it was enough. Without knowing what tomorrow would bring, I knew now it would be right. I went home and slept like a child.

George Otis came over about 2:00 in the afternoon. Shirley and I had been praying, searching the Bible, and looking for some kind of answer. When George joined us he said, "Pat, let me ask you one thing. Have you asked God to forgive you for getting yourself into this mess? After all, this isn't God's doing. It's yours."

I said, "No, I guess I haven't. Hadn't thought of that!"

So he said, "Let's begin our prayer with that, and then let's ask God to put in your mind or my mind the way He wants you to go. You've got half an hour now before you have to be at the meeting."

So we prayed. I earnestly asked God to forgive me for getting myself into the predicament, for not asking His guidance before making such a big step and for ignoring the signs. Then I asked Him what I should do now.

While I was praying, the conviction grew that I should simply tell the men at Tetragrammaton the whole story;

what had happened to me since I made the verbal agreement, and how I felt about it now. Their reaction to this weird tale would be my answer! George had the same conviction; so we thanked God and agreed that this is what I'd do.

Well, I jumped in the car and headed for what had to be the most unusual meeting in the history of the record business. But I had the most amazing feeling of peace, because I felt that at least I was taking my stand, and God could determine the outcome.

I figured they'd react in one of two ways. Either they'd say, "This guy is nuts, get him out of here!" or understandably, "Who are you to pass moral judgment on us? We don't need a chaplain around here!"

Either way, they'd wind up showing me the door, and I'd be free of my commitment.

So the meeting began.

I spoke first. "Guys, let me say first that I'm not the same man that walked in here earlier this year when we made our agreement. I'm changed, and I think you ought to know it."

Then I traced the events of my early life, my early commitment to the Lord and how I had drifted away. I explained that eventually I had put my career first, and was amazed to find I didn't have the answers.

"Nothing much I've done lately has worked out very well," I said. "In fact I may be a Jonah in your midst. Maybe you oughta throw me overboard, before I drag the whole ship down!

"Anyway, I'm changing now; I'm putting the Lord first, and I may wind up doing things that would embarrass you. I may make a Billy Graham movie, or I might do two or three hymn albums in a row. I'm going to be outspoken about my faith, and I'm not really going to be too concerned about my career. I'm going to try to do what God wants me to do. If He wants me to have a career, then I'll have one. If He doesn't, I won't."

I explained my personal feelings about the nude album cover, and the sensational advertising copy that had been prepared for my first record.

"Although I went along with it at the time," I said, "now I realize that for me, it's totally wrong. I don't mean to sound preachy, but I may become a source of conflict with you guys."

By this time I had given them every reason for saying, "Well, who needs this guy? Let's forget the whole thing."

Instead, they all sat in silence. Finally, the president of the company who had been hired by Cosby's partner said, "Pat, I haven't said this to anybody, but I think you're right about the nude album cover. We were dead wrong to do that. I've been feeling really low about it, and now you make me feel even worse talking like you're talking. Not only that, but it's been a financial disaster. . .and as far as the ad campaign is concerned, you can make up your own ads, or we'll let you have a complete 'say-so' in whatever way you want."

Then Roy, Bill Cosby's partner and the driving force behind the company said, "Look, I find what you say very moving. I believe this conviction you have will carry into your singing! We want you with us. I think you'll be a better singer because of this."

I couldn't believe my ears! These guys weren't offended —*they couldn't have been more sympathetic!*

Stunned, I said, "Well, guys, I still have to ask for something that may really rub you wrong; sort of a "morals clause" in reverse! Instead of the company firing an employee, I may ask for the right to leave Tetra if, down the road, the company does things that seem to be casting a moral shadow over what I want to do. I know this sounds crazy, but I feel I need this freedom."

I expected them to say, "Look, enough's enough—that's ridiculous!"

Instead they said, "We understand. You can have that."

Then Roy really floored me: he said, "Why do we have to have a contract of any kind? Jack and I've agreed to all the details, and I am sure he'll remember them. When the time comes to pay royalty, he can remind us what we agreed to. And if at any point, you're not happy recording here—why should we try to hold you?"

This was unreal—it couldn't be; record companies just don't operate this way! Yet as he spoke, the Scripture that Otis and Bredesen had given me three days ago flashed into my mind, "Be not unequally yoked with unbelievers." I still don't know what kind of faith those Tetra men have, but man, they'd made a believer out of me!

Just four days before, on that hilltop, I had vowed that I'd die to my career, if God wanted me to—and quickly He had *tested* me to see if I really meant business! When I proved that I *was* willing to sacrifice the career, in an effort just to obey God, He quickly worked out the problem, with a smooth perfection I couldn't have imagined—and then gave my career *back* to me!

But this was only a glimpse of how good God is. Within only a few weeks I was to see how really great God is, and how much more He knows about my business than I do! I began to record, and with more success than the previous few years; at least people knew that Pat Boone was recording again.

However, get this, during the early part of the summer Bill Cosby and his manager parted company! Without the revenue from Cosby's records, the company quickly went bankrupt. Its assets were optioned by a film producing company which had never been in the recording business, and has yet to do anything with records. If I had signed that contract, which my intelligence told me was the best thing to do, my contract right now could be sitting in the musty files of this film production company and I might have been out of the record business for *five years*—the length of the proposed contract!

Talk about the "Perils of Pauline!" A gracious God, because He knows tomorrow, had caught me just before I plunged off a financial cliff, but only as I reached out in faith to Him.

The Oakland Oaks solution was still some long, perilous months away; but the Tetragrammaton episode and other tests and answered prayers were building my faith for the miracle of the Oaks.

I was really convinced by now that God was going to solve this basketball team problem, and that the solution would defy logic and reason. The nervous peeling on my hands had cleared up. I was facing each day with new confidence; we were studying the Bible or praying with folks at night, quite often. At the same time the financial picture was getting worse every day. My partner and I had lived under this burden now for more than a year!

By the end of September 1969 the total indebtedness amounted to nearly $2.5 million. Business friends, millionaires, who knew about my dilemma all along, since then have told me, "We don't know how you survived under the pressure."

Well, about six months before the solution came, I began to say that God was solving it! My friends would look at me as though I was out of my mind. Meanwhile, my own financial advisors Bill Teague, George Dillman and Glenn Wallace, Christian men, were doing their best to come up with an answer. They tried to interest large companies in buying the Oaks. They attempted to persuade a group of wealthy people to take over the franchise. They tried to arrange long-term financing at banks, until we could make a turn-around in Oakland. They would get close to one of these answers and then strike out, time after time.

My partner Ken went all over the country, even to Switzerland, vainly trying to come up with a solution. Yet the more we struck out and the *worse the problem became,* the more Shirley and I relaxed. We knew the solution wouldn't come

159

until God's own time, and however He solved it, it would be perfect—and He would get the glory for the way in which He worked it out.

Oh, we'd get excited sometimes, when it looked like the answer had come. When it didn't, Bill or Glenn would say, "Pat, we thought we had it. We're sorry, but we'll keep trying."

We'd smile and say, "Don't worry. We know God has this under control."

But it was hard to smile the Monday that the bank sent me a letter itemizing various loans and asking me immediately to send a check for $1,300,000! I was already out $700,000, and to think that I could find another $1,300,000 immediately was laughable. The letter read like the one you might get from the telephone company, "If you have already sent your check, just ignore this notice."

We were sort of numb at first, but by the next day, Tuesday, the pain had set in. We had been so sure that God would intervene but now faith was giving way to "black despair." I'd never known the meaning of those words, but I did now. The faith that had been building up between Shirley and me, suddenly disappeared. I was so low I couldn't look up.

That night George would be having his weekly Bible study and prayer session at his home; Harald would be teaching. But I didn't want to see Harald or George, or anybody. I didn't even want to pray—what good could it do now?

And yet, another part of me was crying out for the comfort and strength of other Christians. In this desperate moment, we needed more than sympathy—we needed believers! Praise God, that hungry part of me won out. When George met us at his door that Tuesday night, he said he was startled by the look on my face. For the first time ever he saw hopelessness.

Shirley and I sat behind the other forty or so people, and holding hands, listened to Harald talk about "The gift of

160

faith."

It was stirring. I agreed with everything he said, but somehow, it hadn't worked for me. Had it? I asked him, as we stood with several concerned Christian businessmen by the swimming pool out back after the meeting.

In a sudden burst of what later proved to be inspiration, Harald said, "Brother, God is not going to let this thing bankrupt you! Now that you belong to Him so completely, His name and yours are linked: He will not let it appear to a cynical world that you turned to God as some sort of escape from tragedy! Pat, He is going to lift this thing from you, even now!"

Right then, by the pool, Harald, George, and another dynamic Christian businessman, Harold McNaughton, laid their hands upon me and prayed. "Lord, God, we ask you for a massive and immediate miracle. You are Jehovah, and You are able. For the glory of Jesus, we ask You now for a miracle!" And on the example of Jesus in John 11:42, even before He called Lazarus out of the tomb He thanked God for hearing his prayer, we thanked God for our deliverance. We went home, literally rejoicing.

On the way, we stopped off at a friend's home. He and his wife are fine moral people and professing Christians, but he knew the Oaks situation, too, and couldn't see any hope for us. He asked about it that night.

When we told him how bad it was, he looked at us with love and pity, as if to say, "You poor, poor people."

We said, "Don't worry about it. We just prayed tonight, and thanked God for solving the whole mess. He's got it!"

The next day my attorneys called for a conference. They asked that Shirley be present because they wanted her to have the picture too.

"Here's what is going to happen," they said. "The Oakland Oaks are going to go bankrupt immediately. Then the creditors will come against your partner and quickly bankrupt him. Next they will come against you. We believe we

161

have a fighting chance to have them attach everything you've got and wait, rather than throw you into bankruptcy. Everything possible will be sold, and then you'll be able to work off the indebtedness over the next five or ten years. We think that's the best we can hope for, and, Pat, we're very sorry."

"Fellas, you've done your best," I said. "We appreciate it. Now that we all give up—watch! God is going to solve this."

They looked up at us as though we were two obsessed, crazy people. They said, "But Pat, you don't understand. It's out of our hands. It's now in the hands of the bank."

We said, "You fellas don't understand. *The bank is in the hands of God.*"

They left shaking their heads.

Two days later the news was on TV and in the newspapers. A man by the name of Earl Forman from Washington, D.C. went to the bank in San Francisco and bought the Oakland Oaks, for close to $2,000,000! I've never met the man, but when I do, I think I'll hug him. As far as I know, he doesn't realize he was part of a fantastic miracle of God, in answer to prayer. But then, neither did Pharoah in Moses' day! In about a week the negotiations were completed and the Oaks moved to Washington where they were renamed the Washington Caps.

Isn't God wonderful? Thank you, dear Clint Davidson. Thank you, David Wilkerson. Thank you, George Otis. Thank you, Harald Bredesen. Thank you, all you bright-eyed, radiant, Spirit-filled people who shared with us the reality and nearness of our God, who is above all, and through all, and in us all.

And above all, thank you, Jesus.

162

CHAPTER 17

WHAT'S HAPPENING?

I've just been reading back over what I've written.

I guess all this sounds pretty incredible, doesn't it? Well, if the whole story seems hopelessly naive, Sunday-schoolish, out of touch with 1970's reality to you, wherever you live and whatever your frame of reference is—imagine trying to make this work in Hollywood, California, in the heart of Glitter City, the movie colony, CBS and NBC, Emmy, Oscar and Grammy races, big-time sophisticated showbiz—the topless, bottomless, soul-less Weathervane of the World!

I'm still an entertainer; but what chance does a guy like me—a "religious nut" as so many think—have in the day of *Easy Rider, The Graduate* and *Midnight Cowboy?*

Good question!

Well, for the first time in my life, I can truthfully say—I don't care!

Oh, I love singing, performing and acting, and want to keep at it, but *only if God leads,* and *as He directs.* I figure that if the bank and the basketball business, as well

163

as electronics and real estate are all in God's hands—so is the entertainment world. And the funny thing is, the less I worry about my career, the better it goes!

For three years I had hounded my agents to get me a dramatic part on TV—anybody's dramatic show. I wanted to remind people that I was an actor, and could handle a dramatic challenge. But they couldn't beg, borrow or steal a part for me. I was a "singer," they said.

Yet, within two weeks after my hilltop surrender, producer Aaron Spelling, Danny Thomas' partner, called me on the phone.

"Pat," he said, "We're doing a movie for TV with Sammy Davis, and we think it's a real winner—a very dramatic thing, private detective. The role of Sammy's partner is a strong one, and we want you to do it."

I read the script, and liked it. I suggested some changes which they went for in a minute, and Aaron said he was glad I thought of them. It proved to be a very highly rated show, and was the ABC Movie of the Week.

The Beverly Hillbillies producer, Paul Henning, called next and asked me to do their show and suggested show-casing my new record! Then Carol Burnett rolled out her red carpet, and after that I hosted a TV special. In the months ahead, plans fell in place for Dick Ross and Associates to produce the movie version of *The Cross the Switchblade* and they offered me the dramatic assignment of portraying David Wilkerson! Now I was filled with the same spirit that enables David and could do this picture without method acting.

The records started selling too, including "Rapture," a new hymn album, my fastest-selling LP in five years!

And suddenly almost every movie I ever made was back on TV. It was incredible. It looked like a "Pat Boone film festival" on TV—and I had little to do with arranging *any* of these things!

My friends would comment, "Say, I saw two of your movies on TV last week. What's goin' on?"

This often gave me the opportunity to tell them what God had been doing in our lives. Of course, now I really had something to talk about! Before I didn't talk about my faith much because I was afraid it would jeopardize my career.

Gradually my manager and public relations people became apprehensive. They said, "Pat, look. You're already thought of as Joe Square in some Hollywood circles. Can't you ease up on some of these appearances like the Campus Crusade film special, the Oral Roberts TV Show, the Rex Humbard appearances, the Youth for Christ rallies? . . .There won't be any parts for you to play! People will be afraid even to make jokes about you because of your religious image."

In a nice way they were trying to say, "Look, you're going off the deep end." And their concern was honest and genuine.

But listen *and believe me,* I wouldn't trade what I have now for all the gold records and Oscars and Emmys in the world!

That's why, when September came and I received the letter from the bank requesting $1,300,000, I laughed. I could look at my hands and see how the "nervous peel" had cleared up. Our family was gloriously together and alive. God was living in our house; He was communicating with us through His Spirit and dramatically answering our prayers.

Everywhere I went, people were wanting to know if God is real. I talked to young kids on the beach at Daytona, to hippies in Los Angeles, Chicago and New York. Ministers especially were interested.

One vital young minister in the Church of Christ, Dean Dennis, had heard rumors about Shirley's transformation. He came as a Christian brother to "straighten us out" doctrinally, to prove to us from God's Word that we'd been misled, misinformed. But when he heard our account of what the Lord had done, and when we re-examined the Scriptures together, *he wept* for the first time, he tells us, in 15 years! He went home to prayerfully study his Bible again.

165

Within a few weeks, he also surrendered to the Holy Spirit and received His gift of a prayer language, though he knew it would cost him his pulpit! He surrendered his career as a preacher to God, and now God has given Dean an exciting, successful new life as an evangelist!

Today, more and more devoted members of our beloved Church of Christ are discovering the reality of the Holy Spirit. Often the first reaction of our ministers is very negative because of excesses, abuses, fakery and fanatacism associated with "Spirit movements" of the past, as well as stemming from honest doctrinal convictions. They are having second thoughts, however, because of the glowing spiritual transformations in the lives of people they know. Can their deep love for God come from the Devil?

The same things are occurring in churches of virtually every Protestant denomination, as well as in the Roman Catholic church.

My friend, Bob Walker, editor of *Christian Life* magazine, tells the story of his visit to Notre Dame University in the early days of the charismatic renewal there several years ago. He met with Dr. Edward O'Connor, head of the department of theology and Kevin Ranaghan, professor of literature at the Catholic Women's College of St. Mary's, also in South Bend, Ind.

The three men spent four hours together that afternoon in a time of rich fellowship in the Lord. Eagerly, O'Connor reported on the remarkable things that were happening among the men at Notre Dame, as well as at Newman Fellowship Halls on Big Ten university campuses. Ranaghan recounted a similar spiritual awakening among the women at St. Mary's, as a result of the new interest in the person and work of the Holy Spirit.

At one point O'Connor said, "I received my doctorate in Europe on the subject of the Holy Spirit. Yet, in recent weeks, I have found myself sitting at the feet of students here at Notre Dame University and learning about the *reality of His presence and power in our day."*

Since then Dr. Edward O'Connor has given this testimony in public many times, and is perhaps one of the outstanding spokesman in the Roman Catholic church advocating that men and women everywhere submit to God and receive the infilling of the Holy Spirit.

Could there be any other hope for achieving the "unity of the Spirit" (Ephesians 4:3) in the religious world today? Can anything but the Spirit of God unite us?

Said John Wesley, famed circuit-riding preacher and founder of the great Methodist Church, "It does not appear that these extraordinary gifts of the Holy Ghost were common in the church for more than two or three centuries. We seldom hear of them after that fatal period when the emperor Constantine called himself a Christian. . .from this time they almost totally ceased. . . .The Christians had no more of the Spirit of Christ than the other heathens. . . . This was the real cause why the extraordinary gifts of the Holy Ghost were no longer to be found in the Christian church; because the Christians were turned heathen again, and had only a dead form left." (Wesley Works, Vol. 7. Sermon 89, pp. 26-27.)

As we were flying down to Miami from New York the other day, the stewardess wanted to talk, and we discovered she was a Catholic. But she was dissatisfied with formality and eager to know more about the Bible, so she squeezed into Shirley's seat beside her.

After we had been talking for an hour and a half, the man in the seat behind us said, "I see you all are reading the Bible and talking about it. I think that's wonderful. May I read something to you in Latin?"

I turned and saw he was a Catholic priest! So I excused myself and sat down beside him. We talked about what the Holy Spirit is doing today in the Catholic church.

"I don't doubt that the Holy Spirit is able to do all that I hear about, but I'm afraid of the counterfeiter," he said. "Satan could lead us to believe things that aren't true."

He was absolutely correct. There are two sources of spiritual influence in the world today: God and Satan. Satan has his spirits, and they're evil spirits. As always, Satan must attempt to counterfeit the Holy Spirit and discredit Him. He will attempt to mislead people into believing in the occult, spiritism of all kinds and witchcraft. *Watch it; it's happening now!* As defense against these tricks of Satan, our only sure guide is the Word of God. Here, and here alone, is the truth which Jesus said will indeed make us free. And in this connection, the Bible says, "Submit yourselves therefore to God. Resist the devil, and he will flee from you. Draw nigh to God, and He will draw nigh to you" (James 4:7-8). In fact, more than ever, we need God's Spirit to help us!

So he said, "I agree with that." Then I told him about our discoveries in the Holy Spirit and what He had meant to us. Each time I mentioned a Latin phrase from Shirley's early prayer language, he knew what it meant and translated it. As we landed in Miami, all he could say was "Remarkable! Remarkable!"

This activity of the Holy Spirit today is drawing Christians together in an astonishing way. Wasn't this the characteristic which identified the Christians of the first century, and distinguished them from the other members of society? In fact, the pagan world marveled when they observed Christians of many races and backgrounds in their fellowship. "Behold how they love one another," they said.

Remember the home Bible study groups that I mentioned Shirley and I took part in? Just last night on TV, Billy Graham referred to these as "Where the church today is going."

We've seen why: friends and neighbors and college kids are coming together, in a warm spiritual fellowship, to get down to the "nitty gritty of life." They want to worship and study in an informal, personal way—to share experiences and pray for specific needs, meeting from "house to house," as in Acts 2:46!

Talk about "group therapy"! These sessions deal with all human needs, right down to the soul level. The tears flow, and love grows where God's Spirit is the therapist! I've referred to Romans 5:5 before, but I want to quote it again. Listen, "The love of God has been poured out within our hearts through *the Holy Spirit* who was given to us." And the more you love God, the more you love others. You can't help it!

You know, Jesus said the second greatest commandment is "You shall Love your neighbor as yourself" (Mark 12:31). We found that God meant just that: He's led us to do things for our neighbors that were beyond our own human natures.

One evening as Shirley, little Laury, a young friend and I were praying we received the very strong impression that God wanted us to go to a neighbor's house and pray for him. We knew he had a fatal disease, and we'd been praying for him already, but this was a shock! We hardly knew him. It was 10 o'clock at night—and he was Jewish!

We had quite a tussle; it was completely against our nature, and of course "It's just not done" in Beverly Hills. We knew he and his family might resent our coming, and if the word got around, we'd be the joke of the town or worse. Still, we decided that we loved God and our dying neighbor even more than we loved our own pride and reputation. So we went!

To our amazement, he seemed touched that we would do such a thing. After their initial bewilderment, as we explained why we had come at that late hour, he and his wife allowed us to pray for him in the name of Jesus. Little Laury put her hands on his chest and prayed her own sweet prayer, and we left him my New Testament. He told us several days later that he'd been reading it, talking to "the

Big Fella," and appreciated our continuing prayers.

A couple of months later, our neighbor died. But we don't think that's the end of the story.

We may not know until we get to Heaven what good was accomplished by that late evening. I keep remembering what Jesus said in Mark 9:37, "Whoever receives one child like this in My name is receiving Me." And the man did just that.

We know two things: God loves that man and his wife and children and we do, too. And at least, we as neighbors did what the Spirit prompted us to do. The rest is in God's hands.

There was also an evening with Wilt Chamberlain.

I don't think Wilt would mind my mentioning the time I invited him over for "the most unusual night of his life." This was in 1969 while he had a cast on his leg, as a result of the knee injury that threatened to end his career as one of the greatest basketball players of all time. Publicly Big Wilt was saying he'd "be back" in time for the playoffs. The doctor way saying, "No." So George Otis and I felt led to invite him over, tell him about our experiences with God, and to earnestly pray that his leg would be healed. Wilt came over, chatted with us until the wee hours, and joined us in prayer.

As he hobbled out our door that night, this proud 7'2" super star said, "Now I know I'll be back!"

And he was. He became the star of the NBA "World Series" and scored 45 points in one game alone! The doctors were amazed.

We have also known the compassion of others in praying for our needs.

The day before Christmas this last year Shirley got up early to wrap Christmas presents. She had an appointment at the hair dressers for 9:00 A.M., and seeing that the time was nearing when she should leave, she lifted the cover of the window seat to put the gifts out of sight until she

170

returned.

Somehow, the heavy cover of the window seat fell shut on her wrist. Immediately she felt excruciating pain and saw that the bone was at an odd angle. She went into the kitchen holding her arm and our cook asked what the trouble was. When Shirley showed her, she exclaimed, "Mrs. Boone, it's broken! I'll call the doctor."

At that very moment John Day, manager of the Valley Christian Bookstore came to the back door with some Bibles Shirley had ordered to give friends for Christmas. John is a Jewish Christian — a "completed Jew," as he puts it — and also has been filled with the Holy Spirit. When he saw Shirley's swollen, discoloring wrist, he said simply, "Let me pray."

Putting his hand on Shirley's wrist, he claimed healing for her in the name of Jesus Christ. Immediately Shirley felt the pain stop. And then, as she watched, the swelling went down, and before their eyes even the deep blue discoloration disappeared! John left singing; the cook and Shirley were gasping for breath. The wrist had been broken, but by the time she had changed her clothes and was on her way to the hair dresser's to meet her appointment, there was no evidence of any injury whatsoever!

Now I know that's hard to believe in this day of modern science. We'd sooner accept that man had transplanted a new arm than that God had healed the old one! But United Press International ran a story May 8, 1970, that was picked up in the Los Angeles *Times* and papers all over the world, about an incident just as dramatic as Shirley's arm!

Ann Turner, 15, of Tilton, Indiana, who'd been totally blinded by looking directly at the solar eclipse March 7, had spent two months in prayer. Three-hundred groups and individuals wrote her they also were praying for her daily, though the doctor had declared her eyes scarred and hopeless.

On Thursday, May 7th, Ann *suddenly could see again!*

"I can see! I can see!" she cried, burying her face in her hands and weeping. Dr. Daniel Thompson, her original specialist, examined her again and declared her vision normal. The doctor said it definitely had not been a case of hysterical or hypnotic blindness, fakery or phobia. It had been physical and actual. He said he wouldn't call it a miracle, but certainly a "medical phenomenon."

"I believe it was a miracle," said Ann's mother.

And the girl who'd been praying in *blind faith* for two solid months, said, "I knew God wouldn't let me down." He didn't—but what if she'd quit praying?

Jesus said in Matthew 21:22, "And everything you ask in prayer, believing, you shall receive." He said this, of course, to disciples. And though God says in James 4:3, "You ask and do not receive, because you ask with wrong motives so that you may spend it on your own pleasures," I'm coming to believe that what we receive from God is often most limited by our degree of commitment and faith.

The other day, for instance, a businessman came to see me from San Diego to describe an invention of his, for which he was seeking financial backers. I wasn't at home when he arrived, so Shirley talked with him at first. Soon, he said quite frankly, "I envy you your talents. I envy you your happy family life. But most of all, I envy you your salvation!"

Shirley saw he was serious, and that he believed he could never be saved. She showed him various Scripture passages which point out that God's salvation is for everyone, even though all of us have sinned. But this man felt it was too late for him.

About that time I arrived with my friend George Otis, and we continued the discussion.

This man proved to be about the most difficult person to convince that God loved him of anyone I ever met! Somewhere in his younger days he claimed that he had rejected God. As a result, he was convinced that he was doomed to

172

spend eternity in hell. You see, he was limiting what God could, or would, do for him!

Despite his curious and dogged determination that he was totally unworthy, and could not be converted to Christ, the Holy Spirit spoke to him through the Bible verses which we read, and the guidance He gave us as we talked. Finally, the man said, "Well, maybe, someday. I sure would like to believe you folks. Please pray for me when I leave." And trembling, he started to go.

But George said, "Then, you admit that you are rejecting Christ now—again!"

He started to say, "Yes," and then broke down and cried like a baby! We threw our arms around him, and sobbing, he dropped to his knees. Eagerly he asked Jesus Christ to be his Savior and rushed to the telephone to call his wife. Through his tears, he exclaimed excitedly, "Jesus heard me, honey. I know it! I've become a Christian."

By now, we were all blubbering. It was beautiful!

The transformation in his attitude and his very being was one of the most astonishing things I have ever seen. Shortly after that, he was baptized in San Diego.

All four of our girls are having their experiences with the Holy Spirit's power, too. In a simple, natural way, they share with their friends at school the excitement that comes from having the Son of God as their constant companion, helping them in every area of their lives.

The other day, Lindy brought a close friend of hers home after school, the daughter of a well-known TV and film producer. Michelle is a wonderful young girl who's been living through some real problems at home. She'd been intrigued by this "extra something" she saw in Lindy and wanted to share it.

Shirley sat down with the girls and they went through the Bible, reading about Jesus, and how He wants to be with and in us all. The more she understood, the more Michelle realized this was what she wanted! Very simply and quietly

Michelle said, "I believe in Jesus. Will He be in me, too?" Joyfully, Lindy and Shirley assured her that He would. Very shortly after this she was baptized in water by a minister, and Jesus baptized her in His Spirit.

Our girls aren't bashful at all about sharing their relationship in God's Spirit with their friends. One afternoon, they invited a Jewish girl friend to join them in their devotion. After prayer, the girls sang in the Spirit, the Lord weaving the words and melodies together. When it was over, the friend was in tears, "That was so beautiful. How did you learn that?" The girls assured her they hadn't learned it!

In two days, she was baptized twice: in Christ's Spirit and in our pool. That swimming pool is a busy place these days We now keep it heated all winter, and not long ago, we baptized five people in one week! In the last year, in our Beverly Hills swimming pool, we've seen Jews, Catholics, Protestants, (blacks and whites) meet the Savior and be baptized in that pool. I don't know if that moves you, but it's absolutely thrilling to us!

When we bought our lovely home in Beverly Hills ten years ago, we did not anticipate how the Lord would be able to use it in His program of bringing people to Jesus Christ.

We always opened it to small groups from our church. Young people like to come here and play badminton and volleyball, and then swim in the pool. Every New Year's Eve we have a hundred or more people in for a party. When the midnight hour arrives we are in prayer, asking the Lord for guidance in the New Year ahead.

In the early days, we even built a large family room with a fireplace for occasions like this. But we little realized then that so many people would come knocking at our door to discover how to learn about Jesus Christ. Now we meet here for Bible Study and prayer. And, of course, we had no idea that we would be able to use our swimming pool in which to baptize people who surrendered their lives to Christ.

Now we ask the Lord to confront all who come into the house with His presence.

Those who don't yet know Him as Savior, we pray will discover how great He really is. Those who have already received Him, we hope will find how much more He can mean to them.

On one of the few afternoons I was at home last winter I went to the door to answer a knock.

It was a handsome Negro about 30 years of age. He identified himself as Bill. He said he had been driving through Beverly Hills and suddenly realized he was passing our home. (It had been pointed out to him some time ago when he was taking a sightseeing tour through Beverly Hills.)

"I just thought I wanted to talk to you," he explained.

I invited him in and we sat down in the den. He told me he had met me once while he worked as a car parker. I had to admit I did not remember the occasion, but I encouraged him to talk.

"Guess I am sort of discouraged. I had worked up to an automobile salesman, then the rug was pulled out from under me. I got another job this morning and start tomorrow—but I can't understand why I have so many ups and downs."

"Well, Bill," I said, "maybe the Lord is trying to show you something. I know what it is to go through hard times."

Then I told him how difficult it had been for me to get jobs several years ago, and how we had almost lost our house. I also told him how the Lord had worked in our lives since then, and how we had come to trust Him.

"I tried to read the Bible several times last year, but it didn't make sense to me," he said.

By this time I realized that Bill really didn't know why he had stopped in to see me. I also have come to realize that when two people get together in a situation like this, that it may be the Lord who has brought about the meeting. So I excused myself and went upstairs where I knew Shirley and two of our daughters, Cherry and Laurie, were. I explained to them the situation. Quickly we prayed that the Lord would give me the wisdom to help Bill put his trust in Jesus Christ.

When we had finished praying Shirley called to him.

"Bill, come on upstairs."

In our master bedroom where we do a great deal of our praying, Bill knelt down with us.

"We believe that the Lord sent you here so you could get close to Him," I said.

"I'm beginning to believe you are right," he replied.

Then I asked him if he knew the story about Philip and the Ethiopian eunuch. He admitted that he didn't. So I opened my Bible to Acts 8 and read the account.

There was an Ethiopian eunuch, a court official of Candace, queen of the Ethiopians, who was in charge of all her treasure; and he had come to Jerusalem to worship.

And he was returning and sitting in his chariot, and was reading the prophet Isaiah.

And the Spirit said to Philip, "Go up and join this chariot."

And when Philip had run up, he heard him reading Isaiah the prophet, and said, "Do you understand what you are reading?"

And he said, "Well, how could I, unless someone guides me?" And he invited Philip to come up and sit with him.

Now the passage of Scripture which he was reading was this: "He was led as a sheep to slaughter; and as a lamb before its shearer is silent, so He does not open His mouth.

"In humiliation His judgment was taken away; who shall relate His generation? For His life is removed from the earth."

And the eunuch answered Philip and said, "Please tell me, of whom does the prophet say this? Of himself, or of someone else?"

And Philip opened his mouth, and beginning from this Scripture he preached Jesus to him.

And as they went along the rad they came to some water; and the eunuch said, "Look! Water! What prevents me from being baptized?"

And Philip said, "If you believe with all your heart, you may." And he answered and said, "I believe that Jesus Christ is the Son of God."

And he ordered the chariot to stop; and they both went down into the water, Philip as well as the eunuch; and he baptized him. (Acts 8:27-38)

"I wanted to share this with you for two reasons, Bill," I said. "One is, that I wanted you to see how God brought two men together for a brief moment in time so that one man might find Christ. It's not likely that they ever saw one another again, as it's possible we may never see one another again.

"The other reason is, that one of these men was black and the other white. You see, there is a real parallel between our situation today and this one that happened in the Bible so many years ago."

We talked a little bit more about what it means to trust Jesus Christ completely.

"That's what I want to do," said Bill. "Then I would like to be baptized like the Ethiopian."

"All right," I said, "you tell Christ that you are giving your life completely to Him as we pray, right now. Then I will baptize you in our swimming pool right outside the door."

He did. Then I gave him a jump suit I keep handy when I baptize people in our pool. And when I put on mine we went into the pool. There he acknowledged again that he was putting his life completely in the hands of Jesus Christ. I baptized him then in obedience to the command of Jesus Himself, and according to his example.

As he was about to leave Bill said, "I don't know how to thank you for what this has meant to me, but God knows . . .And the story you read from the Bible about Philip and the Ethiopian means more to me than you realize. *You see,*

my grandfather came from Ethiopia, so I am an Ethiopian,"
he said.

But the story didn't stop there. The next day Bill brought
his wife and their five children for a visit. Shirley spent some
time talking with her, and discovered she was on a spiritual
search as well. Before many hours had passed, Bill's wife
said she wanted to put her trust in Jesus Christ as Savior and
the Lord of her life. That evening I baptized her in the pool.

Like many others, this incident has been a beautiful
demonstration to us of how real the Bible can become when
we search it for applications to our own lives. I am convinced this is what God wants us to do even in this 20th
century.

Ever ask yourself why the first century church inflamed
the whole known world in just a few years? I'll tell you why.
Folks were going from house to house saying, "Wow, something's happened to me! I've got to tell you. I've just found
out about Jesus, and He lives!"

Today this is happening all over again in the 20th century.
People are going from house to house sharing their experiences, relating what God has done with them, through them
and for them.

God is alive *today*. He is working in the lives of people
today, just as He did in the days of the Bible. The Word of
God is plain: "Jesus Christ is the same yesterday, today, yes
and forever" (Hebrews 13:8).

Wherever I go, I find that people are discovering this
fantastic truth themselves—Jesus lives! They're not interested in church history. They're not even interested in
creeds or the new building budget. They want to know how
God can change their lives today. Is He interested in their
finances? In their health? In their family relationships?
Whether they're poor, or black—or both? We have
discovered that He is, and God can change things, brother!
Starting with you!

We know, because He changed us.

Now we realize that only He can touch and change others. We can't do it; we can't make other people carbon copies of ourselves, though we tried to do it for years. No, we're freed from the pressure of "doing something for God." He does it; we're simply His witnesses. We can plant, but some-one else may water, and a third person may reap. This new freedom is a beautiful thing to us.

But unless "something's happened" to *you,* you don't have much to plant, do you?"

CHAPTER 18

THE NOW PEOPLE

When I wrote my first book, *Twixt Twelve and Twenty,* I was barely out of my teens. I was addressing myself to the problems that kids had then. The temptations in those days, in addition to the age old sex urges, were to drink and smoke. Today it's goof balls, marijuana, LSD, heroin. No longer is it just the body that kids are gambling with, but the mind as well.

Parents once could say, "Well, I messed around a little bit myself when I was young."

The idea was that even if a young person sowed a few wild oats, he'd soon settle down. Not so today. Those who experiment with narcotics can become hopelessly addicted for life, become mindless vegetables, may even die. Some authorities claim that *one "trip" on LSD* may affect four generations of children born afterwards!! And, of course, we know that some children born to LSD users have had exposed spines, two heads, and other gruesome physical deformities. Some children are *born addicted to drugs because of their parents' habits!*

The shocking fact is that one estimate claims *40 per cent*

of all university students either are already on drugs or have experimented with them.

In the face of these terrifying facts, how can a parent counsel his children? Or what attitude should a young person take who wants to stay in tune with what's happening in his world?

As I write this, I have just returned from New York City where I've been filming *The Cross and the Switchblade.* The film story of David Wilkerson is centered in Harlem and Brooklyn. In many of the scenes we worked with non-professional performers—some of whom were plainly on drugs right then! In talking with these ghetto kids I was amazed at their apprehensions about the future. They appeared to have a premonition of some giant showdown ahead. . . .

Young people everywhere appear to be "bugged" by the frantic pace, the inequities, the double standards of life. Frustrated by the monstrous institutional world looming over them, they strike out blindly in dissent and riot. But unmindful of their own strength and uncertain of the future, they also give voice to their fears.

Their music reflects their anxiety. A very recent No. 1 song is *In the Year 2525.* It suggests that by that time we may not be alive. A song by Peggy Lee asks *Is That All There Is?* Another doleful number carries the title, *Dooms-Day.* The Cowsills, who recorded the number one record of *Hair,* followed it with *The Prophecy of Daniel and St. John the Divine.* This was pure Bible prophecy set to music—about the last days of the world!

Credence Clearwater, on his big number one record, *Bad Moon Rising,* warns again and again that he hopes we are ready, for the end of all time is near.

The Blood, Sweat, and Tears group has a number one record called *When I Die.* One line in that song fitfully attempts to deny both heaven and hell, but fearfully acknowledges both Satan and demons.

Now, you can't dance to this complicated record; you can only listen. And our kids *are* listening!

In the Bible, both in the Old Testament and the New Testament, a great day of judgment is predicted. And when Jesus' disciples asked Him when that would be, He said: "See to it that no one misleads you. For many will come in My name, saying, 'I am the Christ,' and will mislead many. And you will be hearing of wars and rumors of wars; see that you are not frightened, for those things must take place, but that is not yet the end.

"For nation will rise against nation, and kingdom against kingdom, and in various places there will be famines and earthquakes.

"But all these things are merely the beginning of birth pangs." (Matthew 24:4-8).

A great, growing number of young people today see in their own culture this coming time of judgment! A new record by Credence Clearwater is called, *It Came From the Sky* in which he alludes to the Lord. Another hit song suggests a meeting with the Lord in the air.

As a result of this apprehension, many young people are saying that somehow or another—if He's real—*they must find God.* Some of the hippie communes, where groups of boys and girls live together in remote areas under primitive conditions, claim they are turning themselves over completely to religion. Arlo Guthrie, author of *Alice's Restaurant,* a big hit movie and record, is one of the folk song heroes of the young people. In an article in *Life* magazine he listed the Bible as one of his favorites for reading. Donovan, the mysterious Scottish balladeer who recorded *Mellow Yellow,* admitted publicly that he had been on drugs because they were the "in thing." But, he added, this is not really "where it's at. Drugs are not it; there's got to be something else."

Even folk-poet Bob Dylan has publicly and musically

183

turned from social protest to songs urging an individual search for spiritual identity and for personal union with the source of all things[1]

These young people are searching for *reality*. The church, as they see it today, doesn't have it. They see its failures, double standards, lack of concern and are turned off. Even much of what we call "evangelical Christianity" has way too little to offer them. Because doctrine, no matter how pure or correct it may be, *is not enough*. At one demonstration here on the West Coast recently, young people carried signs that read, "Christianity, no! Jesus, yes."

They are not satisfied with the organized forms of evangelical or orthodox Christianity. These, to them, are words and rules. But they do respond to a person who is walking evidence that life with God does indeed have meaning — that it's exciting and real. *And they are intrigued with this person, Jesus.* When anyone can talk about a personal experience he has had with Jesus, kids will listen. They're hungry and thirsty for spiritual reality. Why, they even wear what they call "Jesus boots," sandals like they imagine He wore 2,000 years ago!

Paul Stookey, member of the well-known singing group, Peter, Paul and Mary, a human conglomerate of hit records, is a good illustration. In his search for reality, Stookey became a Christian. This is where life began, he says. But when he became filled with the Holy Spirit, then life truly became real and exciting for him. Now everywhere the group goes, from college campuses to concert halls, Paul steps to the mike alone and says, "I just want you folks to know I'm singing for Jesus now."

That's all he says. *But that communicates!*

What's happened to Paul Stookey has been so dynamic that it's influenced many others. Peter Yarrow, the other male member of the group, turned up unannounced and unexpected at a Campus Crusade for Christ TV special because Paul was there leading a bunch of kids from UCLA in a spontaneous sing-along.

He said to the huge group of college kids and to the whole nation by television: "I'm Jewish, but I just want you to know that I'm turned on to Jesus too."

Then he led the Campus Crusade for Christ group in singing "Jesus, Pray for Me."

Often, after their concerts, Paul will hold private sessions with groups of young people. He'll play a number of songs he's written about God, share with them what he's found in the Bible and how real Jesus is to him. They'll just sit and "rap" (as they describe their conversations), expressing their doubts and confusions.

Finally, after he's explained what it really means to put one's faith in Christ and the Word of God, Stookey says, "Would any of you like to know my friend, Jesus?"

Invariably many of them say, "Man, I'd like to."

Then he says, "Let's quietly sit here and pray. Let's invite Jesus to come where we are."

Paul has a tender, sensitive spirit. But he's *direct,* too; no time for games. And one by one these kids will begin to weep, kneel and give their lives to Jesus. They have no hang-up about it at all.

I saw this demonstrated in a youth meeting the other night at Anaheim, Calif. David Wilkerson, the author of *The Cross and the Switchblade,* had spoken to 8,000 young people. Nobody talks straighter to kids than David does! When he finished, he invited them to meet him in another room if they wished to commit their lives to Jesus Christ. About 400 did, and I went along to see what would happen.

Many were high on drugs of all kinds. But they were earnest, eager. They had tired of everything—and I mean everything. Some of those kids have lived a lifetime in 17 years! Some were younger—14 and 15 years old. But now they were weeping as the Holy Spirit convicted them of their need to acknowledge Jesus Christ as their Savior.

I was particularly interested in one boy because, as we learned later, he was "freaking out" on LSD. I don't know how he ever got to the counseling room, because it didn't appear that he could have heard what Wilkerson had said. He didn't seem to know where he was, or what he was doing.

When I arrived he was sitting on a chair writhing, contorted, clawing at his face and moaning. All around, other kids were sitting on chairs or on the floor. Some were kneeling. Many were weeping. I could hear them saying, "I want Jesus. I want to be free of this stuff."

Wilkerson again told them what Jesus had done as the result of His death on Calvary and His resurrection from the dead 2,000 years ago.

"You're going to be *free* tonight because Jesus will meet you," he told them.

As I watched the boy who was on LSD, two of Wilkerson's assistants walked up behind him, put their hands lightly on his shoulders and began to pray quietly. By now his contortions were more grotesque than ever, and his groanings could be heard around the room. If the boy was aware of the hands on his shoulders he couldn't have known the men were praying—because they weren't praying aloud! His eyes were closed and he really seemed oblivious to everything around him.

But, as they prayed, suddenly he slumped down in his chair. His head fell forward and he dozed off, utterly relaxed. The men pulled the chair against the wall and went around talking and praying with others *just as if they had fully expected this to happen!*

I knew I had seen another miracle. Afterwards I talked to Wilkerson. When I told him what I had seen, he smiled.

"You don't think we'd be here if we didn't know the power of prayer, do you? God is real, and we've seen Him do a lot more miraculous things than that."

I was deeply stirred. Where had I been all my life? Since then, I've seen so many other young people, to whom religion was just words, also "turned on" when they saw that Jesus is alive, and that the Holy Spirit will demonstrate this to them when they commit their lives to Him.

Like Chip, our 15-year-old friend, who came over to our home early last summer with his guitar, to sing with our girls. They got to talking about God, and Cherry, our oldest daughter who's about his age, told him about Jesus. He took her about as seriously as if she'd been talking about Santa Claus.

But he kept coming back to play tennis, and to sing folk songs. Cherry wept more than once because of Chip's cynicism and unwillingness to accept her testimony about Jesus. He couldn't yet accept what she was saying but he saw something "different" in her.

Then one day he called to ask if she would help him with his guitar. She almost refused because she didn't think she could take his sceptical attitude any longer. But he came, and that day he referred to Jesus as a bastard; though he didn't say this disrespectfully. He had simply decided that Mary must have had an illegitimate child. When Shirley came home they were still talking. I returned still later and joined the conversation which lasted until 1 A.M.

Chip believed that Jesus was an "extra good man," but not the Son of God.

I said, "Chip, either Christ was what he said He was—or the greatest liar and con man in history! But we *know* Him! He's our friend."

As we talked I could see that while he understood many things, he was still hazy about "living with Jesus." I asked him if he had actually read what Jesus said; he hadn't. So Cherry gave him her modern language New Testament after another long talk. *In four days*—he had read it, asked his mother if he could be baptized, and returned again! He was really "turned on"!

He didn't want to go to a particular church, so a minister friend, John Day, baptized him in our swimming pool. Chip's whole life changed; he was literally a "new creature." On the way to church with us one evening, he said, "This may sound silly, but I don't get much out of those church services.

187

If I go out to the golf course close to our home, take my guitar and make up songs to Jesus, I really feel close to Him. Is that silly?"

"Chip," I said, "if that's silly. . .David, the King of Israel, was silly, because that's exactly what he did when he was a boy. He went out on a hill and took his version of a guitar. The songs of God he 'made up' became our Psalms in the Old Testament. And the Bible says that *David was a man after God's own heart.*

"Now, if you can take that kind of spontaneity, that kind of feeling into the worship service with you when you go to church, surely God will cause that kind of spirit of communicate to *others,* because *everybody today needs that kind of* feeling, that *communion* that you have with God on the golf course."

That was only the beginning for Chip.

A few weeks later he had gone with us to hear a brilliant young evangelist and Bible teacher, Kenneth Copeland, talk about faith. For many years Chip had been plagued with an asthmatic condition. It had become so severe that he was forced to attend a private school in Arizona, and to spend much of the rest of the year with relatives in Palm Springs where the climate is dryer. This meant separation from his parents who lived part of the time in Beverly Hills and the other part in Washington, D.C. where his father was an important diplomat and businessman. So Chip would come home for vacation to hack and cough his way through summer and finally go back to the desert when school started. Now. . .after he surrendered his life to Christ and began this adventurous walk in the Spirit. . .one day Chip was chatting with the Lord, having a real "rapping session," singing and praying at home alone.

"Look Jesus," he said, "I've got this asthma. I don't have to have this asthma, do I? I want to live here at home with my family. So, Jesus, I ask You to just take this asthma away, I claim Your promise in Mark 11:24 and thank You in Your name."

As summer wore on the hacking coughs disappeared! At the end of the summer he went to the doctor.

"This is amazing," said the doctor. I don't see any trace of asthma. Why don't you enroll in school here and stay as long as you can?"

Chip is still in school here and has had no problem with asthma. But that's not all. Shortly after that he injured his knee and it became very painful.

The doctor put on a cast, but when he removed it, the knee was still swollen and painful.

"Chip," he said, "I hate to tell you this, but you've got arthritis in your knee. It's unusual for a 15-year-old, but your tennis and running days are over. You must not aggravate it or you may become a total cripple."

God had answered Chip's prayer before. As he thought and prayed about his knee, he could see no reason why God wouldn't come to his aid again. As he understood it, the promise was in God's Word. For Jesus had said, "Therefore I say unto you, all things for which you pray and ask, believe that you have received them, and they shall be granted you" (Mark 11:24). And, by now Chip had plenty of faith to "believe"!

He told me what happened several days later. He was wearing shorts that day as he looked down at the swollen knee and said, "Jesus, Lord—look, I've been reading where You were afflicted with all my diseases, that you 'bore my infirmities,' and that with Your stripes I am healed. I don't have to have this knee business, do I? This arthritis?"

Then talking right to Satan, he said, *"Leave me alone! In the name of Jesus, get out of my body!"*

Finally he turned to God again, "Lord Jesus, thank You for healing my knee."

The pain left immediately! And as *Chip watched, the swelling in his knee subsided completely.* He ran out on the golf course and jumped up and down. He laughed and shouted and sang. Eventually, when he returned to the

189

doctor for an examination before going back to school, the physician said, "I guess your knees are still giving you trouble, aren't they? Remember, when you get back in school you must not play tennis or run."

"But doc, I play tennis every day! I run all the time. My knees are okay!"

"Chip, I told you this could result in permanent injury," the doctor insisted.

"Doc, I don't know how to tell you this, but just to put it bluntly, God has healed my knees completely."

The doctor remembering Chip's last visit, said, "I have already decided that the asthmatic condition of yours was "psychosomatic." But in this case, you have actual damage to your cartilage! Let me get my x-rays and show you."

When the physician tried to put his hand on the knees where the damage had been on Chip's knee, he simply could not locate it! Finally, he put his x-rays away and said, "I just don't understand it."

I understand it. Chip understands it. The apostle did, too (Phil. 4:13, 19; II Tim. 1:12).

What happened to Chip is typical of what is happening to thousands of young people across the country and around the world today. They have been "turned off" by formal religion, the institutional church. They see it simply as a collection of buildings and an oppressive, out-of-date agent of restraint to their human desires with little to offer but ritual and dry rules. They want no part of it.

But—when they discover that the institutionalized "church" of today may actually have obscured the vibrant reality of the person of Jesus Christ, they eagerly turn to Him. They suspect that the materialism of modern society has failed utterly. But in Jesus, the humble carpenter who identified with human beings on every level, who healed the sick and filled all the empty spaces with His love, they see the hope for *their* day. So, in multiplying numbers, they cry, "Jesus, be *my* Savior; be *my* friend!"